# Praise f[or]

"Horses are magnif[icent] beings. Noted Reiki [...] is a perfect way to connect peacefully with horses in a heart-to-heart way using 'compassion through mindfulness' and focusing on 'being, not doing.' Using case studies, Ms. Prasad shows how the five Reiki precepts — leaving anger and worry aside and being humble, honest, and compassionate — can heal both human and horse in deeply reciprocal ways. By dissolving boundaries of separateness it is simply amazing what can be accomplished as we rewild and reconnect with other animals. I highly recommend this book to anyone who wants to learn how to connect with horses and all other animals. Reiki can be that expansive and deep."

–Marc Bekoff, Ph.D., author of *The Emotional Lives of Animals* and *Rewilding our Hearts: Building Pathways of Compassion and Coexistence.*

"Heart To Heart With Horses: The Equine Lover's Guide to Reiki by Kathleen Prasad is a wonderful continuation of her previous Animal Reiki book, *Reiki for Dogs: Using Spiritual Energy to Heal and Vitalize Man's Best Friend*. With case studies, personal anecdotes, meditation practices, and deep insights, Kathleen's new book takes us on a journey into the heart of the system of Reiki. I recommend this book to any horse lover who would love not only to support horses in their healing, but who also wants to go deeper into their own personal spiritual journey. In fact, many of the teachings in this excellent book are not just for horse lovers, but also for all human beings who want to open their hearts to a more compassionate world."

–Frans Stiene, co-founder of The International House of Reiki and author of *The Inner Heart of Reiki - Rediscovering Your True Self.*

"From the moment I held Kathleen's manuscript in my hand, I felt the love, passion and power pour from the pages. Few animals have worked themselves as deeply into our culture and psyche as the horse. Offering Reiki is an amazing way not only to help heal, connect and develop a deeper connection with horses, but your own heart and soul as well. Thank you, Kathleen, for offering yet another amazing book! This book belongs in every horse lover's library, but is best kept within close reach, as it is a book to be referred back to often."

–Lisa Ross-Williams, Publisher/Editor-In- Chief
*Natural Horse Magazine* and author of the award
winning book, *Down-To- Earth Natural Horse Care*.

"Heart to Heart Healing with Horses: The Equine Lover's Guide to Reiki is a moving, gracefully written book filled practical wisdom. Kathleen Prasad's combination of personal and professional anecdotes will tug at your heartstrings as you learn how to employ the now scientifically validated practice of Reiki to enhance the health and well being of your horse's body, mind and spirit."

–Linda Kohanov, author of *The Tao of Equus*,
*Riding Between the Worlds*, and *Way of the Horse*

"This book is a MUST-READ for all animal lovers. In current times our world is becoming more aware of the healing power of energy. We're learning to see and hear with our hearts rather with our eyes and ears, and to view the world from a more compassionate and spiritual perspective. Horses have long mastered these skills and in this sensitive and captivating book Kathleen shows us how eager they are to help us progress. Kathleen leads us into the wonderful world of horses, showing them to be our ready and willing spiritual partners, enthusiastic to share their numerous gifts. Many short case studies and compelling quotations from acclaimed pundits help us to further understand the countless life lessons awaiting us in the equine world.

*Kathleen also takes us through the looking glass of her own life, health challenges and spiritual growth. Heart To Heart With Horses will be enjoyed by anyone who has ever loved an animal of any kind."*

—Gail Pope, founder, BrightHaven Holistic Animal Sanctuary, Hospice, Rescue and Education Center, Brighthaven.org, Author, *Soar My Butterfly: The Animal Dying Experience* and *The BrightHaven Guide to Animal Hospice*

"I am honored to write an endorsement for a book on the concept of Reiki for horses. I started the Remus Memorial Horse Sanctuary over 30 years ago and am extremely proud of the work that we do including work with elderly horses, including Shane the oldest horse in the world who died at 52, and our work with blind horses. We embrace holistic therapies in our work with these animals. Reiki is used as part of our synergistic approach to helping these horses who have come from awful backgrounds where they have suffered the most appalling emotional and physical cruelty and torment. As a calm hands-off experience for the animals, Reiki totally compliments our philosophy of respect and compassion towards these wonderful, elegant creatures. Our history was borne on their backs, and it is pleasing when they have reached their twilight years that we are able to give them something back to help them including a home of safety, respect and Reiki.

I have seen Kathleen work at our Sanctuary and with our animals and I wholeheartedly support her work and her philosophy and therefore totally endorse this book. I know the seventy plus horses at Remus and the other animals would totally agree with me!"

—Sue Burton, founder, Remus Memorial Horse Sanctuary

"This novel book dedicated to spiritual healing of horses through the meditation and touch of Reiki is remarkable. For many of us, we are familiar with Reiki practitioners that use actual touch to heal (hands-on healing). In her book, Kathleen explains that Reiki involves two modalities for healing, namely, meditation to establish the heart-to-heart connection of spiritual energy, and light touch to convey compassion and care in nurturing the heart-to-heart connection. For horses in particular, meditation alone can provide healing, but for many, it is the touch that enables the very strong connection to healing. Reiki is also a means to convey compassion through mindfulness. In this form of practice, Reiki becomes spiritual healing rather than the more surface aspects of touch. Through meditation, it produces a state of inner peace and self-healing. Further, through healing horses, they in turn heal us by sharing unconditional acceptance. Finally, Reiki is a state of being rather than doing. With many case examples that follow the precepts of: Do not anger or worry, and be humble, honest and compassionate, this book is a "must read" for all of us involved in animal healing."

–W. Jean Dodds, D.V.M., founder of Hemopet

# HEART TO HEART
## With
# HORSES

The Equine Lover's Guide to Reiki

KATHLEEN PRASAD

Foreword by Allen M. Schoen, D.V.M., M.S.

Text Copyright © 2017 Kathleen Prasad. All rights reserved. No part of this publication may be reproduced, stored in a retrieval system, or transmitted in any form or by any means without the prior written permission of Ms. Prasad, nor be otherwise circulated in any form of binding or cover other than that in which it is published.

Published in the United States by
Animal Reiki Source, San Rafael, CA

ISBN-10: 0-9983580-0-2
ISBN-13: 978-0-9983580-0-0

Production and Cover: www.Damonza.com
Interior Photographs: © Lexie Cataldo (www.InJoyPhotography.com) and Adobe Stock.

DISCLAIMER: The suggestions in this book are not intended as a substitute for professional veterinary care. Reiki sessions are given for the purpose of stress reduction and relaxation to promote healing. Reiki is not a substitute for medical diagnosis and treatment. Reiki practitioners do not diagnose conditions nor do they prescribe, perform medical treatment, nor interfere with the treatment of a licensed medical professional. It is recommended that animals be taken to a licensed veterinarian or licensed health care professional for any ailment they have.

*For the soft and gentle hearted,*
*May you awaken to your true healing power...*

# CONTENTS

**Foreword:** . . . . . . . . . . . . . . . . . . . . . . . . . . . . . . . . . . . . xi
**Introduction:** What is Healing? . . . . . . . . . . . . . . . . . . . . . xix
**Chapter 1:** A Brief Introduction to the System of Reiki . . . . . . 1
**Chapter 2:** My Horse Teachers . . . . . . . . . . . . . . . . . . . . . . . 19
**Chapter 3:** Peace + Love = Healing . . . . . . . . . . . . . . . . . . . . 29
**Chapter 4:** Healing from Within . . . . . . . . . . . . . . . . . . . . . 35
**Chapter 5:** Horses as Teachers . . . . . . . . . . . . . . . . . . . . . . . 53
**Chapter 6:** State of Mind . . . . . . . . . . . . . . . . . . . . . . . . . . . 63
**Chapter 7:** Three Ways to Nurture Your Horse's Spirit, and Your Own . . . . . . . . . . . . . . . . . . . . . . . . . . . . . . . . . . 77
**Chapter 8:** Healing Fear and Finding Courage . . . . . . . . . . . 93
**Chapter 9:** Ways to Meditate . . . . . . . . . . . . . . . . . . . . . . . 109
**Chapter 10:** Heart to Heart Connections . . . . . . . . . . . . . . 121
**Chapter 11:** Guidelines for Sharing Reiki with Your Horse . . . . . . . . . . . . . . . . . . . . . . . . . . . . . . . . . . . . . 129
**Chapter 12:** Communication and Reiki . . . . . . . . . . . . . . . 147
**Chapter 13:** Saying Goodbye . . . . . . . . . . . . . . . . . . . . . . . 159
**Chapter 14:** How to Radiate Reiki . . . . . . . . . . . . . . . . . . . 173
**Chapter 15:** The Healing Power of Compassion and an Open Heart . . . . . . . . . . . . . . . . . . . . . . . . . . . . . . . . . . 187
Index of Meditations . . . . . . . . . . . . . . . . . . . . . . . . . . . . . . 190
Acknowledgements . . . . . . . . . . . . . . . . . . . . . . . . . . . . . . . 191
About the Author . . . . . . . . . . . . . . . . . . . . . . . . . . . . . . . . 193

# FOREWORD

Animal healing has come a long way since the early 1980's when it was primarily limited to conventional medicine and surgery. As one of the pioneers in holistic integrative veterinary medicine, I have seen many of the complementary therapies that have been used on people be transposed onto animals. Some of these approaches have been able to be extrapolated over to animals with great success and others not as much. There is debate as to whether some of the results of various therapies in people may be due to what is commonly known as the placebo effect. One of the benefits of seeing therapies work on animals is that this placebo effect is largely removed, though it may still be present. For example if the human caretaker of the animals would like to see improvement despite the reality of the animals condition, one might claim to see the animal better, but in reality they are still suffering or in pain. This is one of the benefits in evaluating the effects of various complementary therapies to see whether a therapy is truly beneficial or not.

As a veterinarian trained in the scientific method, I have been taught to the point of indoctrination that one must only trust what can be observed, measured, tested and reproducible in double blind placebo controlled trials. This is a typical view of western medical professionals. I am appreciative that appropriate training in western medicine and surgery is a great and an essential foundation for offering the best in health care. Yet, early on in my career, I became fascinated with exploring additional complementary therapies to help animals that either could not be helped by medicine and surgery or were having side effects from them. My passion was to evaluate complementary therapies that might help animals even more. This led me to take advanced training in acupuncture, botanical medicine, nutritional medicine, supplements, manual therapies such as chiropractic care and osteopathy as well as various approaches to energy medicine. I began to question the status quo and felt it was essential to keep an open mind when exploring additional therapeutic approaches. I realized that it was important to maintain a balance of open mindedness, yet not to an extreme of gullible belief in anything that claimed beneficial effects. I also realized that no one form of medicine had all the answers or cures, but that we needed to study, evaluate and develop a more expansive, integrative and holistic approach to healing, integrating the best of all therapies in order to offer the greatest opportunities to help animals and people heal. It simply seemed to make the most sense to create a more integrative approach.

Recently it has also been acknowledged that many so claimed "scientific studies" and "clinical studies" were being funded more and more by medical companies that had an inherent conflict of interest in the outcome of the studies and would either cease funding if the studies were not coming out with their intended results or would not fund independent studies. In addition, it was becoming more challenging to find independent funding to support needed research in the various therapies. It became too difficult and too expensive to support studies that did not have a potential for patents of a particular medicine, procedure or approach.

In order to properly evaluate whether a particular therapy is truly beneficial, I have found that I evaluate them based on a few simple criteria. First I see if there are sufficient successful anecdotal cases that warrant further evaluation. I then look at if the results are reproducible in a significant number of patients. I then explore what the scientific basis of the therapy might be and what research there is to document them. These questions are certainly a bit more challenging to explore when dealing with more subtle energy healing modalities such as Reiki. If I find that a particular approach meets these criteria, I feel like it may be worth seeing if it can be of benefit to an animal when nothing else is working.

This has been the primary theme of my veterinary and personal journey exploring the question "What is ultimate healing?" This question has guided my life's journey. When I began to study and integrate complementary therapies, I first began with looking at modalities that I felt had the best scientific documentation available in order to adequately address the concerns of conventional veterinarians. This is what led me to begin with acupuncture and botanical medicine. During that time I did come across Reiki healing, which was quite new in North America and actually took the initial training in it in the early 1980's. At that time I felt that even though I resonated with the concepts of Reiki, it would be too challenging to differentiate the benefits of it from the placebo effect. I integrated Reiki into my overall approach without talking about it too much. For the benefit of getting other therapies more accepted, I focused my attention on complementary therapies that would be easily documented.

During the past few decades I have seen Reiki healing evolve in various forms, some positively and some negatively. Unfortunately, I must admit, I have found that certain "Reiki healers" were marketing Reiki as a modality that could heal or help almost everything. Though there may be some truth in that it can be of some benefit, my concern is that there were certain individuals who were marketing themselves as healers and that they did not need western medicine or complementary therapies and that Reiki could heal all illnesses just as well. The challenge with that perspective and marketing approach is that some people would then naively believe that they would pay for Reiki healing for their animals when the animal really needed either medicine, surgery or other more efficacious and documented complementary therapies. This became more popular as certain "self proclaimed healers" would then expand upon this and add more and more questionable healing modalities to their approach and then one would not know what therapy was having what effect, if anything at all. This in turn prevented or delayed animals from receiving appropriate veterinary medical attention. I feel that this has led to a very questionable reputation for "Reiki healing" in general. When one proclaims themselves as an amazing healer rather than honestly explaining the concepts of Reiki, I feel it does a serious disservice to true Reiki.

This unfortunate situation has led even myself who has been quite open-minded in integrating complementary therapies, to be quite skeptical and jaded in what has been sometimes marketed as Reiki. Yet, I also have seen it to be quite beneficial in some patients, when only Reiki has been used by a competent, appropriately educated and trained individual that are aware of its indications and limitations and not trying to dissuade someone away from other therapies that might be more appropriate at the time.

It is this paradox that has led me to respect certain individuals who practice Reiki and be rather skeptical of others who appear to "market" it well to the detriment of the animals. I suggest that animal caretakers ask: "what is the most appropriate approach or combination of approaches to help an animal heal" and not be attached to a particular modality. As I mention previously, my philosophy is that no one form of medicine has all the answers and an integrative approach incorporating the most beneficial therapies seems to offer animals the best opportunity to heal.

This leads me to explain why I agreed to write a forward for Kathleen Prasad's book on Reiki. When Kathleen asked me to write the forward for this book, I was quite reticent and resistant to the idea. Yet, I sensed her sincerity and commitment and felt that it might be worthwhile to at least talk with her about it all. After a Skype session and realizing where she was coming from regarding her Reiki training and her approach, I agreed to review the manuscript and then see if I felt it was appropriate for me to write a forward.

Throughout the book Kathleen has shared many Reiki experiences and techniques, along with her explanation of what Reiki is based on her training. Once I read Chapter 1, which offers a brief introduction to the System of Reiki, I appreciated where Kathleen was coming from and the benefits the book could offer to readers. I also deeply appreciated the quote by her teacher, Frans Stiene that she begins the chapter with: "From a traditional Japanese perspective we can say that Reiki means our True Self, and the system of Reiki is a system that helps us to remember our True Self/Reiki again." That is what I felt when I took my initial Reiki training decades ago: that it allows for an awareness that it is not something "we do" but that when we clear ourselves of all of our programming, our beliefs, our egoic tendencies, we are simply a vessel for an "energy" that can have beneficial effects. I have come to appreciate that there are subtle energies that we may not have the ability to measure or completely understand at this time. This does not mean that may not be of some benefit.

In my book *The Compassionate Equestrian* (Trafalgar Books, 2015), I share my thoughts on what I consider ultimate healing is for horses. I review all my different theories and perspectives on what I feel are the best approaches to help horses and their human caretakers heal. My co-author, Susan Gordon, a holistic horse trainer, also shares her perspectives based on her decades of experience in training horses. We share our beliefs that the ultimate healing of horses is to heal the hearts and minds of riders and equine caretakers. We offer different approaches including time for quiet, focused intention, which seem quite similar and overlap with some topics Kathleen describes in this book. I was pleased to see the complementary approaches. The essence of all healing is loving-kindness and compassion for all beings. The key is to be love, and all else emanates from that. That is also one of the essences of the teachings of Reiki.

While teaching veterinary acupuncture and meditation in Japan, I had the benefit of being able to visit the original home of Reiki and appreciated the beauty of the place. I appreciate Kathleen's explanation of Reiki and how she emphasizes that Reiki begins with the individual and our own personal healing journey. This is key to the true essence of Reiki, healing ourselves first as much as possible prior to being of benefit to others.

I feel that this book can be of great benefit to the practice of Reiki, to horses as well as to Reiki practitioners. It is the best explanation of Reiki that I have read. Kathleen Prasad is an excellent writer, sharing from her own training, her own personal journey and from her heartfelt experiences.

She shares how loving kindness and compassion are the keys to all healing.

This is truly the essence of all healing.

My hope is that her writings will be of great benefit to all who read this book.

Allen M. Schoen, D.V.M., M.S., Ph.D. (hon.)

Holistic, Integrative Veterinarian, Author, Philosopher

*The Compassionate Equestrian* (Trafalgar Books, June 2015)

www.drschoen.com

马

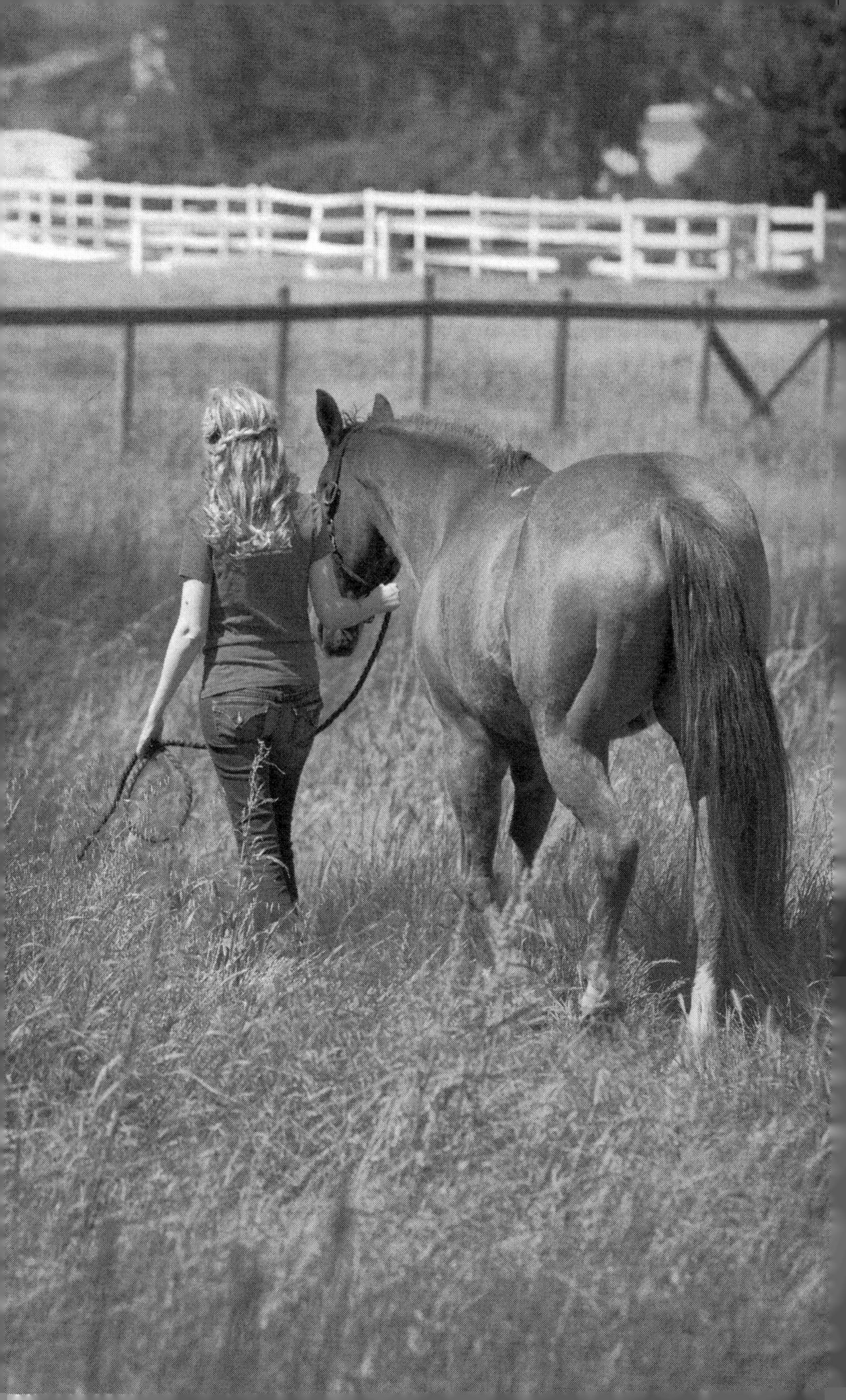

# INTRODUCTION
## What is Healing?

*"There's a difference between healing and curing. To be cured means to be free of disease. To be healed literally means "to become whole," which means to repair inner fractures, restore emotional harmony, and attain peace, which can happen even in the presence of disease."*

—Lissa Rankin

### The healing dream:

*The hills spread out before me as far as I could see, miles of the green rolling hills of a California Spring, dotted with strong oaks and orange poppies. I stood at the top of the ridge astride my chestnut quarter horse, Shawnee, surveying all below me. Bareback and bridle-less, we began our path down the hillside. As the incline lessened, we began to pick up speed. Soon we were cantering joyfully through the wildflowers, up and down gentle grassy hills, the sun at our backs all the while. The feeling of limitless space and easy friendship filled my heart with joy.*

*I awoke with a start to the dark walls of my room. A strong surge of nausea filled my entire being; I could not lift my head off the pil-*

*low. Then I remembered: I was pregnant and very ill; I had been in bed for almost two months. I shut my eyes and tried to go back to the dream, but it was gone, as easily as it had arrived. Still, the memory lingered inside me like a little light of hope. I knew I would get back to myself, to the light of the sun, to my beloved horses. I would get back...*

MY DREAM OF riding Shawnee returned to me several times during that dark phase, when I spent almost three months in bed from morning sickness, too ill even to sit up. This recurring dream of lightness and freedom as I rode Shawnee across the hills was one of the few instances of relief from suffering I experienced during that time. It was many months later, while visiting Shawnee in the large retirement pasture where he now lives happily with his herd, that I realized that this recurring dream was no coincidence, no random vision.

The weather was strange that day: heavy downpours and wind that alternated with periods of sunny calm. As I stood with Shawnee in the dappled sun, a rain cloud suddenly opened above us and poured down a freezing rain as the wind picked up. I huddled against Shawnee's side and waited for the squall to stop. I felt his warm shoulder beneath my face. I realized that standing here, sheltered from the wind behind his steady back, the weather didn't feel cold. I didn't have the feeling that I needed to get out of the rain at all. In fact, I felt completely content to stand in the storm amidst the herd with my wonderful friend. It was at that moment that the memory of the recurring dream came back to me. I hadn't thought of it in many months, but suddenly there it was in my mind, as clear as day. I remembered the feeling of joy and freedom that my friendship with Shawnee had given me in the dream and was filled with thankfulness.

Just then, Shawnee turned his head to nicker softly and nuzzle me. The serenity and peacefulness of his nature embraced my soul, and I felt our hearts connect for a moment with love and gratitude. I realized very clearly that those dreams were a gift from him to me, just as his physical presence had always been. How I had missed being with him when I was ill! Yet he *was* with me then, because two hearts that love one another can never be parted. I leaned on Shawnee and thanked him for the dreams that had brought me relief during my illness. Although I had not able to visit him for those several months while I was so ill, he had found a way to visit me. Now that is real horsepower: the power of our horses to heal with their hearts! When they do so, they mirror back to us our own heart's potential.

Sometimes when we are sick, our illness is all we can see. We begin to identify ourselves with this illness, and it becomes who we are. The peace and joy I felt while connecting with Shawnee in my dream was a very important reminder that my sickness need not define my experience of living. Although at that time I was experiencing intense suffering in my body, in my dream I was able to be completely free, whole, joyful, and peaceful. This helped me to remember my true heart: my spirit, my soul. No matter what difficulties I may face, my heart is never tainted, never broken, never lost, never weak. This deepest part of me is bright, pure, strong, eternal. This inner, spiritual heart existed before I was born into this body and will continue on long after it leaves my earthly shell for the next part of my journey.

Shawnee is now twenty-nine years old. I found him when he was fifteen, and immediately fell in love. I was looking for a safe trail horse, and Shawnee lived at a farm where my friend had moved her horse. Shawnee's person, although she loved him dearly, had become too sick to look after him. She was so touched by how taken I was with him that although she wasn't planning to give him up, she agreed to sell him to me. Shawnee was a kind gentleman through and through, and had been worked too hard and too long in his young, cow-herding ranch days. His front feet looked as though he had foundered at some point in his life and his hocks were stiff with arthritis. Others wondered at my decision to take on his physical issues. Didn't I want a healthy young horse with no problems? I understood their concerns, but when I looked at Shawnee, all I could see was his beautiful heart and gentle nature, and how safe I felt with him. Looking back now, I guess I was just seeing his true being, his spirit and soul.

Knowing the power of Reiki to heal, I knew it would help Shawnee. With Reiki sessions several times a week he did very well—beyond the vet's expectations—and we rode together for four years. I tried other supportive holistic treatments for him, such as acupuncture and chiropractic, but he always got terribly annoyed at all the fuss being made. "Mom, I'm fine!" he seemed to be saying to me. Luckily for me, he enjoyed our quiet Reiki time together and always felt strong and sound when I rode him. I was always careful never to overwork him, and I knew that the best thing for his arthritis was to move. Eventually, Shawnee's advancing arthritis made him too uncomfortable for me to ride him anymore, and so I made the decision to retire him to pasture. I missed our days riding hills and trails together, and even winning a ribbon or two in the ring. Yet I knew it had been the right decision for both of us. He seemed happy to just relax in the pasture with his friends, and we could still keep our heart to heart connection through grooming time, quiet walks side by side, and of course, Reiki.

In looking back on the dream from my time of illness, I realize that more often than not, when we help our horse companions to heal, they find ways to heal us back, even if we don't realize it until much later. I had supported Shawnee through our years together with love and Reiki, and he supported me with the power of his heart when I needed him most, bringing me healing through what he knew I had loved best in our years together:

our rides on the trail. The healing animals give us may be as dramatic as lowering blood pressure, healing depression, and assisting our special needs, or it can be as subtle as a nose on the hand, a kiss to the face, a quiet day on a trail, or even a dream or memory of being together.

Healing our hearts is something horses do effortlessly. I believe it is partly because of who they are in their bodies on this part of their journey: They are close to nature and the earth, deeper in the flow of spiritual energy, and more aware of the impact intention and heartfulness—living with the compassion of open-hearted presence—has on our healing. Animals are pure in heart and pure in intent. Because they live in the moment every second of every day, they have no muddy swirl of emotion or regret, guilt or deception in their hearts. So when we connect with our horses in trust, love, and healing, we are able to witness the brightest sparkling diamonds of clarity, connection, and gratitude. Horses are a shining inspiration for the way we should always be in our world.

This is what the system of Reiki is really all about: remembering our inner light so that we can heal our hearts and spirits, even if our bodies and minds are going through difficulties. The heart is always perfect, always peaceful, always compassionate, and always strong and well, no matter what outer circumstances we face. This is the deeper spiritual truth that is revealed when we practice the system of Reiki with our horses.

Sometimes we let our illnesses, injuries, or physical and mental limitations define us. We think to ourselves, I *am* this or that problem, this or that limitation, this or that negative situation we are going through. Unfortunately, we often do the same to our horses when they are going through something difficult. The truth is, it is not the difficulties we face that make us who we are, but rather the way we handle them. We can let ourselves be discouraged or even give up when the going gets tough, or we can look deeper and remember the bright light that is our true heart, our courage, and our perfection even in the hardest of times. In the same way, we can choose to see only what is "wrong" with our horses, or choose to see the blessings in each moment. When we remember our true hearts, we can find the strength to rise up to meet challenges with grace and dignity. When we do so, our horses can lean on us when they need us most.

It is hard to remember how perfect our inner spirit is, especially when someone we love is sick, or we ourselves suffer, and this is where the practice of meditation can get us back on track. All of the teachings of Reiki help us to go more deeply into a meditative space so that we can remember the power and purity of our hearts. In this deep meditative space, healing and peace can easily flow. For me, practicing the system of Reiki with animals (in other words, meditating in various ways with animals) has been the strongest support I have found in helping me navigate life's greatest challenges. Along the way I have learned so much about what true healing means from my horse teachers.

I've titled this book *Heart To Heart With Horses: The Equine Guide to Reiki* in honor of my horse friends, and all the blessings I have received through heart connections with horses. This book is my testament to the real power of horses in our lives! Throughout history, mankind may have admired the physical strength or "horsepower" of equines, but perhaps we have overlooked the even greater inner horsepower that our equine friends embody: the power to heal through compassionate, heartful connections. This healing power of the heart is something that we humans also possess! It is through sharing Reiki meditations with horses that I have gained an awareness and deep appreciation of the healing power that lies within the heart of each of us. When we as humans come forward and connect with horses in this beautiful heart space, it is a transformational experience that will heal and change us both, and ripple out into the world.

In this book, I hope to reveal how you and the horses you love can access heart to heart connections through Reiki for true and lasting healing. I'll share Reiki tips and lessons about healing that I've learned from the horses in my life, as well as some inspiring case studies from other Reiki practitioners about horses who've been healed with Reiki. To help you get started right away, I've also included several Reiki meditations for you to share with the horses you love.

Take a moment now, and set your intention to open your heart to infinite healing possibility: let's travel together through these pages to a new level of harmony and well-being. Let's discover what heart to heart connection can mean for our own healing and for the healing of our horses. Sharing Reiki with our horses can help us to remember that the healing power of the heart is truly infinite!

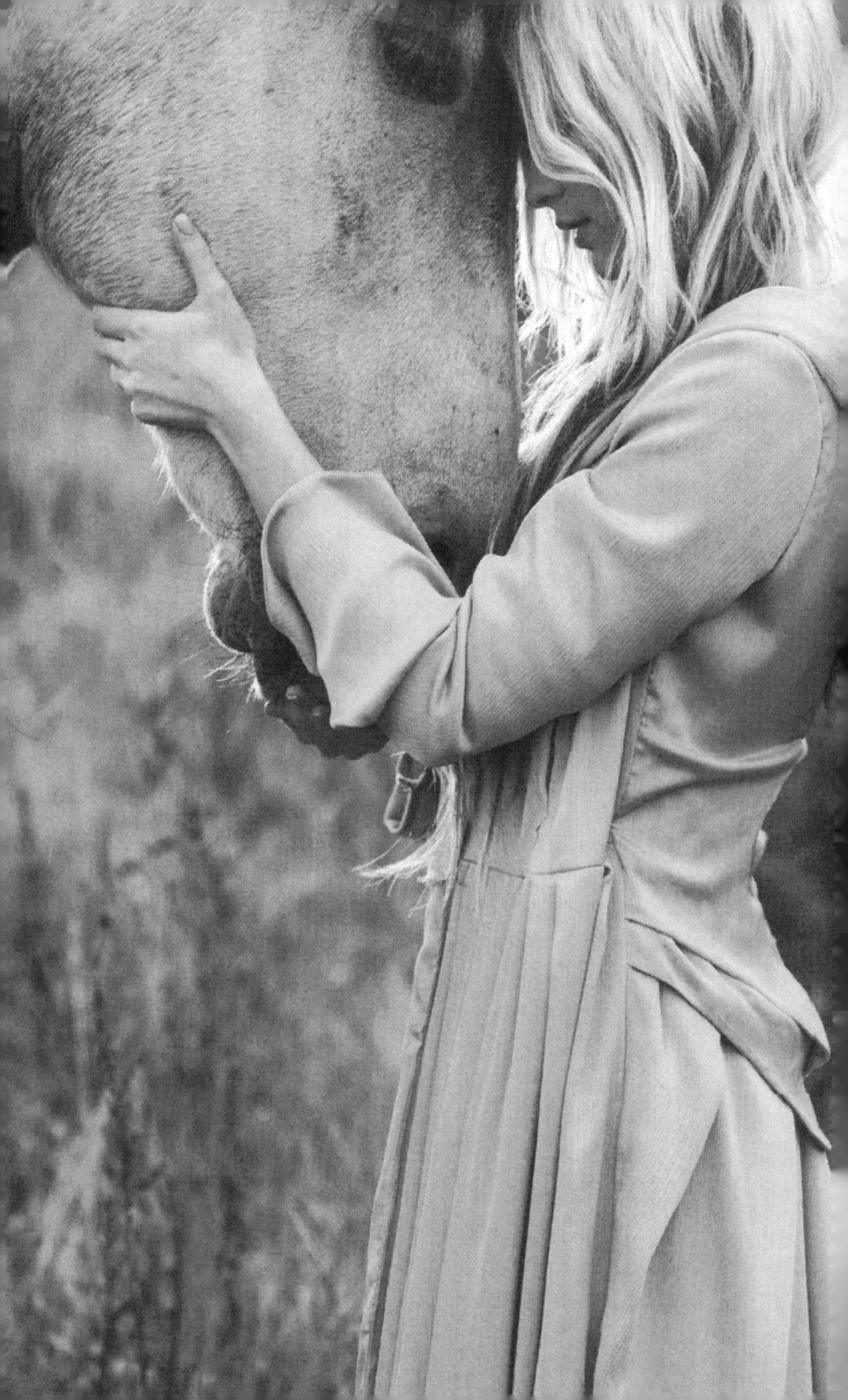

# CHAPTER 1
# A Brief Introduction to the System of Reiki

*"From a traditional Japanese perspective we can say that Reiki means our True Self, and the system of Reiki (Usui Reiki Ryoho) is a system that helps us to remember our True Self/Reiki again."*

—*Frans Stiene*

ARIEL IS A shy gray mare at BrightHaven Sanctuary in northern California. She was rescued from the Mexican rodeo circuit, and has many scars that bear testament to her difficult past. She is now living a peaceful life where humans require nothing from her, and she can just be a horse and live in her herd. Yet due to her history, she is extremely untrusting of humans. When she first arrived at the sanctuary, she would stand very far from my Reiki students when we would come out to the pasture to share meditation. Even though she wouldn't physically approach, she would watch us very carefully, her ears pricked at attention, showing lots of interest in what we were "doing" while we were meditating.

One morning, I decided to go out to the pasture to meditate

alone before my students arrived. The morning was warm, sunny, and quiet—the perfect meditation space. I stood outside the fence, closed my eyes, and began my Reiki meditation. I opened my heart to the horses in the pasture. After several minutes I felt as though someone was watching me. I opened my eyes, and sure enough, Ariel had walked all the way across the pasture and now stood just outside my reach, staring right at me. I placed my hands, palms up, just inside the fence and continued my meditative breathing. I could feel a beautiful, peaceful atmosphere all around us. Another of the horses, a paint named Mocha, walked up to my hands, touched them with her nose, looked at Ariel as if to say, "See how safe she is?" and walked away. I noticed several other horses in the pasture had come closer and stood in various poses of napping and relaxation. It seemed as though they had all come forward to show Ariel how to connect in this meditative space.

Ariel had watched Mocha's approach very carefully, and was clearly keeping an eye on her herd members for direction. Slowly, Ariel took one step closer to me, then stopped and watched the other horses. Then she took another step: still her companions dozed and relaxed. Finally, she very slowly stretched her neck toward me, eventually touching her nose to my palm. She jerked her head upward as if she could not quite believe herself—she had actually approached this human for physical contact! I continued to breathe and meditate peacefully, and she returned her nose to my hand, this time resting it gently in my palm, her eyes slowly closing.

In that beautiful moment, I felt many things: I felt deep peace and contentment enveloping both of us and radiating out into the whole herd. I felt my heart opening so wide with love for Ariel, for the trust she was giving me. I felt immense gratitude for the support of her herd in bringing us together. I felt happiness that she had found her way to the safety of BrightHaven. I felt a bright hope and deep inner knowing that she would learn to trust humans again. There was so much in that moment, and yet there was no movement, no sound, and no words.

This experience was a true "equine Reiki moment." In other words, it was a moment in which a lot was going on, and yet nothing was going on! It was a moment of being present with a horse, with an open, grateful heart and with compassion, but without judgment or worries about the past, without trying to do something to "fix" a problem. It was a time for potential, not a time to push Ariel into what I thought she "needed" to do. When we learn to share peace with our horses, rather than pushing our healing agenda onto them, amazing things can happen!

This is what the practice of Reiki will help you to do: to connect with your horses in a way that makes a deep and lasting healing possible. Ariel has continued to make incredible progress, and shows more and more joy in her life and trust in her human caretakers at BrightHaven. What a brave, bright spirit she is!

In order to help you to be able to create a similar "equine Reiki moment" with a horse you love, let's take a moment to discuss what Reiki is and how practicing the system can enhance your own well-being, as well as help horses to heal.

### *Reiki is a system, and Reiki is spiritual energy*

The name Reiki, pronounced *ray-key*, comes from the Japanese words *rei*, meaning *spirit*, and *ki*, meaning *energy*. Another translation used by my Reiki teacher, Frans Stiene, is True Self. So we could say that the word has two meanings, referring both to a Japanese system of meditative techniques and to our True Self.

You can see both of these meanings reflected in Ariel's story. The story starts with a specific state of mind and meditative practice that I have learned from the system of Reiki. In addition, the connection that occurred through this practice is one in which Ariel and I each were able to shine the light of our True Self, our inner essence, which contains so much love and compassion and peace that all healing possibility exists within it.

In this book, I will use the term Reiki to describe various meditative practices to help us to remember our True Self (which is comprised of spiritual energy and which I like to call our "true heart") in order to achieve healing. I will share many stories of how these specific practices have helped to illuminate the true heart of both the practitioner and the horse. I have found over many years of practice that sharing these Reiki meditations with our animals brings profound peacefulness. Meditating with our horses is a simple path to achieving wellness for all.

As you can see from Ariel's story, meditating with our horses helps us cultivate compassion through a profound depth of connection. When we connect heart to heart with another being, we remember the ultimate truth of existence—that we are all One. This is the place where healing starts. I like to call this "the Reiki Space." It is a place we *remember* rather than something that is new to us, because our hearts already know that we are all connected on this planet. This kind of profound connection is a part of our ancient wisdom, although we may have forgotten it in our attempt to "civilize" ourselves. Our animals are often more in touch with this truth than we are, as they are still so connected to the earth and the laws of nature. Connecting heart to heart with our horses in meditation is a key that can help us open the door to experiencing our True Self or spiritual energy. Within this profound space of energetic heart connections, many wonderful miracles of healing can take place.

## *Reiki is healing touch*

Two parts of the system of Reiki incorporate touch: self-healing and assistance in the healing of others. Reiki practitioners are taught formal hand positions to use when doing Reiki on themselves, as well as hand positions for sharing Reiki with other humans. Because we are very tactile creatures, we humans feel support and compassion in a very direct way through touch. Human clients often describe feelings of relaxation, harmony, and well-being after a Reiki session. When sharing Reiki with horses, it's best to consider touch optional, and use it only when horse-initiated. As in Ariel's case, horses are generally very clear on whether, when, and where they like to be touched.

When our horses choose it, Reiki may involve direct physical contact in the form of light touch on areas of the body that our horses are comfortable with. Thus, each practice will look unique based upon the preferences of each horse. Although Reiki is just as effective without this direct contact, for many horses, the power of touch is a very strong way to convey compassion and care while nurturing a heart to heart connection.

## *Reiki starts with you*

The practices of the system of Reiki help us, step by step, to learn how to hold a space of balance and peacefulness within ourselves, even in the midst of a chaotic or troublesome situation. At first we learn how to maintain an inner balance and calm while we meditate, sitting or standing quietly and undisturbed. In time and with practice we will see this calmness gradually spread out into other areas of our lives, when we aren't formally "practicing." In essence, the peaceful space that meditation creates will begin to follow us wherever we go. Our horses will sense this, and benefit from it also. I call it the "Reiki ripple effect"—when we practice sowing the seeds of open-hearted compassion and peacefulness in ourselves, over time we see the fruits of healing, contentment, transformation, and renewal in our lives.

## *Reiki is compassion through mindfulness*

The most common depictions of Reiki I have read and seen are focused on the surface practices of Reiki as a "hands-on healing" modality for helping others heal bumps and bruises, and indeed that is where I started in my own practice eighteen years ago. Over the years, however, the animals I have connected with have challenged me to let go of these more surface aspects of "curing" and focus instead on the deeper teachings of Reiki and the healing of the spirit. The heart of Reiki practice is about meeting our horses' healing challenges with grace and surrender while we learn to listen to and be present for them in this very moment, in a compassionate space. We must learn how to meditate with our horses for peace with whatever will *be*, instead of pushing onto our horses our own energy, intention and agenda for what we *want*. This is what I like to call "being Reiki"—experiencing an openhearted mindfulness with our horses—and it brings with it amazing healing responses.

## *Reiki is peacefulness*

Because horses are so sensitive to our inner states, when we learn through meditation to create an inner state of balance, almost immediately we can see our horses respond by also becoming calmer and more peaceful. Self-healing can most easily happen when we are truly at peace, and we can see our horses heal themselves much more easily when they, too, are peaceful. In addition, learning to connect with our horses from this calm inner space will also help deepen our relationship with them. Species differences seem to melt away in the Reiki space of a peaceful heart. Peace is an energetic language beyond words, one that horses already understand. They are ready to speak it with us; we just have to remember to listen. The quieter we can become, the more we can hear. To practice Reiki with our horses is to learn how to "Be Peace" with them.

## *Reiki is meditation*

Reiki is a system of spiritual meditation that utilizes practices such as:

Contemplating the Reiki precepts
> "Just for today: Do not anger, do not worry, be humble, be honest, be compassionate."

Practicing traditional breathing techniques

Sharing healing sessions

Visualizing and drawing symbols and chanting mantras

Offering initiations to Reiki students

If we take a deeper look at each of these practices, we can see that at the heart is an intention to create a meditative state of mind:

**Precepts:** When working with the precepts, the key is to contemplate them in a meditative way, so that we can go deeper into their meaning and purpose in our everyday lives, bringing change and healing to all that we do. It is very important to remember that the precepts are about a state of mind, not a set of actions.

The heart of Reiki is this state of mind, for when we are *living* the precepts, we are connecting to our True Self, and healing will happen naturally.

***Breathing techniques:*** When working with the breathing techniques, the key is to follow the breath into a meditative space where healing can happen. Breath is the bridge between the body and the spirit; therefore, we must learn to connect with our breath in order to begin the healing process at the deepest layers of our being.

***Sharing healing sessions:*** As practitioners, if we want to share healing with a person or animal, the key is connecting heart to heart. To do this we must go deeper into a meditative state of mind, which can support the healing process. Often people use the word "treatment" for this experience, but I think this is a very loaded term, and perhaps not the best one to use. The term "treatment" creates a feeling of separation, implying that one being is now the "healer" who is giving something, and the other has something "wrong" or is lacking something. Thinking of the relation between spirits in these terms nurtures ego and negativity. The most effective Reiki healing happens when all of these judgments and separations disappear and we remember that we are all One: all perfect, beautiful bright lights in our true essence. I like to call this process "sharing Reiki," for this invokes more of the sense of connection that is at the core of Reiki practice. Since everyone involved can experience the peacefulness, compassion, and love that Reiki brings (as well as the healing that follows), not just the "client," this is a meditative experience that is experienced and participated in by all, not "given" by one to another.

***Symbols and mantras:*** When practicing the system of Reiki with symbols and mantras, whether through visualization, contemplation, or chanting, we learn that they are tools to help us to release our busy minds and find our inner "still point," or inner meditative space, to facilitate healing.

***Initiations:*** Reiki teachers learn to share a healing ritual when meeting with our students called an *initiation*. The intent of an initiation is to create a meditative space of open-hearted connection, a peaceful, compassionate space that also will support the student's healing process and spiritual journey.

Both teachers and practitioners of the system of Reiki often describe how their Reiki meditation practice has healed their lives—from the inside out—and made their world a better and more peaceful place. Our horses appreciate and are drawn to the peacefulness of the meditative state, and enjoy being our meditation partners. The more we practice, the stronger is this peaceful atmosphere we are able to create for ourselves and those around us.

## Reiki is an equine-assisted therapy practice

When sharing Reiki with horses, practitioners often find an amazing result—we see that the horses are helping *us* to heal, even though we may initially think we are there to help *them* heal. This is a result of the beautiful gift of their presence. Just being with our horses is healing—connecting with them through petting, speaking to them, or even just sitting with their gentle presence has an immediate healing effect on us. This is because horses are fully present, without expectation, judgment, or agenda. They accept us unconditionally as we are, and this causes our hearts to open without our even trying (and sometimes without our even being aware of it). It is when our hearts are open that healing can truly begin. In this way, horses are also mirroring to us the best part of our True Self. Even better, they show us when we've got it right by manifesting their relaxation and connection with us. The more we relax into that peaceful space, the deeper they will relax with us. The more we feel healing within ourselves, the more we will see that they are experiencing healing as well, and so on.

## *Reiki is a state of being, not doing*

The system of Reiki teaches us to let go of our agendas, the feeling of time pressure, our desires to force and to fix—we can simply stop, open our hearts, and *be* with our horses. This sounds very simple, doesn't it? But actually it is quite difficult. What it really means is that we have to be completely and utterly present in the here and now. Our first instinct might be to run from difficulties, hide from suffering, or shift our focus into anger over the past or worrying about the future. Or we might put all our efforts into trying to change what is. So stopping ourselves in the midst of all our intellectual and emotional gobbledy-gook is not that easy. This is why the practices of Reiki are so powerful. With the open heart and compassionate presence that meditation brings, we can see attitudes, situations, and emotions all shift towards balance, understanding, and acceptance. Be patient, be Reiki, and healing will happen!

## *Reiki is ideal for healing horses*

Reiki's effectiveness is not dependent upon physical contact. The practitioner does not manipulate or direct the healing process: the horse connects with and accepts Reiki in the way that is most comfortable—either hands-on or from a distance, or a combination of the two. Because Reiki is essentially a meditative practice, it is easy for anyone to try and it can do no harm, even when practiced by a novice. The stronger our own peaceful state of mind is, the deeper the responses we will see in our horses. Reiki is about connecting to the subtlest of energies—our energy of mind and heart—and thus it touches the deepest source of our essence (True Self) and always supports a path toward balance and harmony. We don't need to focus on what is "wrong" with a horse (in fact, we should always keep our thoughts positive!);

simply by meditating and creating a space of peaceful connection and compassion, profound healing shifts toward balance on all levels of being can happen.

The heart of the system of Reiki is the five Reiki precepts for balanced living, as taught by the founder of the system, Mikao Usui. These precepts are not only the foundation for self-healing in the system of Reiki, but can also be used as guides when working with our horses.

> Just for today…
> Do not anger.
> Do not worry.
> Be humble.
> Be honest.
> Be compassionate.

To understand these precepts more deeply and see how they can help us share healing with our horse companions, let's take a look at them more closely, one by one.

1. *Do not anger.* Horses can live long lives, and for this reason may be entrusted to many homes and guardians throughout their lifetimes. We may sometimes see the results of past abuse or neglect when working with horses, especially those who have come to us later in life. We can begin to feel ourselves becoming very angry about how a horse was previously treated, what he had to go through, and so on. This anger will merely distract us from our primary goal, which is to help the horse. If we

are angry, our horse will sense this and will not want to connect with us.

Reiki meditation helps us to see deeper into the heart of our horse and see his potential for healing, which will make it easier to work through any difficulties we face with patience and calm. Approaching our horse with inner peace rather than anger will help everything will flow toward healing much more easily.

2. *Do not worry.* Over years of working with horses, we might find ourselves dealing with many different kinds of health problems, both physical and emotional. As we nurture horses toward healing, we may find ourselves worrying: about other problems that might manifest, about the expenses of treatment, about how and whether the horse will be able to fully heal from illness and injury, and so on. Worrying about things beyond our control is not helpful.

It's ok to observe the things you are worried about, the things about the situation that frustrate you, or any other bothersome thoughts and emotions. Just don't hold onto them too tightly. Imagine these thoughts and emotions transform into clouds in the sky. Watch them float away. Just let them go without judgment. Your horse will be drawn to the peace that surrounds you as you learn to let go.

3. *Be humble.* Working with our horses can bring us back to humility. In many ways, horses are so much more sensitive than we are to the lessons of healing and life, and we have much to learn from them. Our horses can become some of our most profound spiritual teachers. Reiki practice helps us to open our hearts, to hear what they have to say to us.

4. *Be honest.* Horses require absolute honesty—they just won't accept anything less. We must learn to be completely present in the moment with them, because this is how they live. Reiki practice supports us in meeting them in that mindful place; it is there that we can most easily be who we are with a truthful heart.

5. *Be compassionate.* Developing a relationship with a horse teaches us to dissolve the boundaries of separateness. It teaches us to work together and develop a partnership that transcends species and language. This partnership may begin with groundwork and riding, but at some point will likely also encompass a health challenge. Through this partnership we will learn that in reality we are not so different from our horses, and compassion will grow.

Reiki techniques help to bring balance, calm, and a sense of deep connectedness to and open-heartedness with our horses. When we become aware of this connection, the automatic by-product is an overwhelming sense of well-being and compassion. It is this compassion that is the heart of meditating with horses. To be able to stand with a horse who may be suffering in this deep, peaceful, and compassionate space is the most profound kind of healing we can ever offer to him, or ever to experience ourselves. True, lasting healing is about peace of mind and heart, and this is what sharing Reiki with our horses is all about.

## Case Study: *Jet*
## by Allison Chun

Jet is one of the therapy horses at Haku Baldwin Center in Makawao, Maui, Hawaii, a nonprofit that offers free therapeutic horseback riding lessons for special-needs children. I am a volunteer for this program, and Jet is one of my favorite horses because he is always so careful when he has a child on his back; he is fully aware that he is carrying precious cargo. One day he started limping and was diagnosed with an injured suspensory ligament in his right hind leg—a very serious and potentially crippling injury. He was taken out of the program and put on stall rest but he kept getting worse. Soon his other leg was bothering him more than the injured leg because he was leaning on it heavily to compensate for the injury, as horses do.

I had been sharing Reiki with Jet about three times a month as a volunteer, and another practitioner was coming in about as often to do massage. Jet's vet check at the end of summer was not good. The barn manager started preparing everyone for the eventuality that he might need to be put down. He could not just be put out to pasture, because if he ran around and further injured the ligament, he would be in a tremendous amount of pain as well as permanently crippled. His quality of life was also questionable. He was confined to his stall at all times and in obvious pain. An agreement was reached to reevaluate during his December vet check and make a final decision then.

I started sharing Reiki with Jet five times weekly on average, both in person and remotely. The massage volunteer had stopped working on Jet, so he was only receiving Reiki. I shared Reiki with Jet throughout the autumn until his December vet check.

I have almost no knowledge of horse anatomy or injuries, so I didn't try to direct Reiki toward his injury—I didn't even know what his injury was. I was also concerned about his quality of life, and didn't know if it would be better for him to transition out of his current corporeal body or if we should keep trying more medicine and painkillers. When I practiced Reiki, I asked Jet to share it with me to help him do whatever it was he wanted to do—to get better or to transition on his own or to let us know he wanted help transitioning by not getting better. I didn't want him to suffer or to hang on just because we humans weren't able to let go of him. I had no idea what would be best for him, so all I could do was stay open and trust that he would accept Reiki and use it to help him do what he needed to do. I couldn't hold any expectations, because I didn't know what to hope for!

I was working at the horse center on the day of Jet's December vet check. We trotted him down the length of the barn and back. The vet, a very stoic and understated guy, looked and sounded very surprised. Jet looked much improved—in fact, Jet looked pretty good! Everyone was stunned. Jet was put on a daily rehab exercise program. It was a long recovery period, but after several months Jet started working again in the riding program. I am full of gratitude to the system of Reiki for enabling me to share healing energy with Jet, and to Jet for teaching me so much about trust, openness, and the magic of letting go of expectations!

## Reiki Practice: Horse Hatsurei Ho with Precepts and Affirmations

*Note: This Japanese meditation has been adapted from the practice of Hatsurei Ho as taught by the International House of Reiki. Hatsurei Ho is a Reiki practice used to develop one's spiritual energy. This practice helps develop the *hara*, the energy center located in the lower belly, below the navel. Focusing on the *hara* is a central practice of Japanese Reiki, and assists with energetic grounding, centering and balancing.

1. Stand near your horse(s), keeping your eyes open with a soft focus. Place your hands palm over palm on your lower belly (your *hara*).
2. With each inhalation of breath, feel the energy coming in

through the nose, moving down to the *hara*, and filling the body with a beautiful, healing light.

3. On the exhale, expand the light out of your body through your skin and continue to expand the energy out into your surroundings.

4. Repeat Steps 2 and 3 for several minutes.

5. Place your hands in the *gassho* position (palms together in front of your heart). On the inhale, begin to bring energy into your hands. Feel the energy move along your arms, down though your body and into the *hara*.

6. On the exhale, visualize energy moving from the *hara* back up through the body and then to the arms and out through the hands.

7. Repeat for several minutes. Then return your breathing to normal and sit in the space of energy for a few minutes.

8. When you are ready, relax your hands at your sides and set the intention that you have an open heart to share peace and healing with your horse.

9. Recite the precepts and corresponding affirmations below three times; invite your horse(s) to share this space with you for healing. This is a very gentle intention: simply open your heart to connection.

10. Visualize each precept entering your heart as you inhale. As you exhale, imagine the manifestation of the precept (the affirmation) expanding infinitely out from your heart and into the universe. Open your heart to your horse in this beautiful space.

    Precept: do not anger; Affirmation: loving-kindness

    Precept: do not worry; Affirmation: courage

    Precept: be humble; Affirmation: surrender

Precept: be honest; Affirmation: joy

Precept: be compassionate; Affirmation: harmony

11. Stay with your horse, relaxing your mind and heart into the beautiful space of connection, for as long as you like. When you are ready, thank your horse for connecting with you and set your intention to finish your practice.

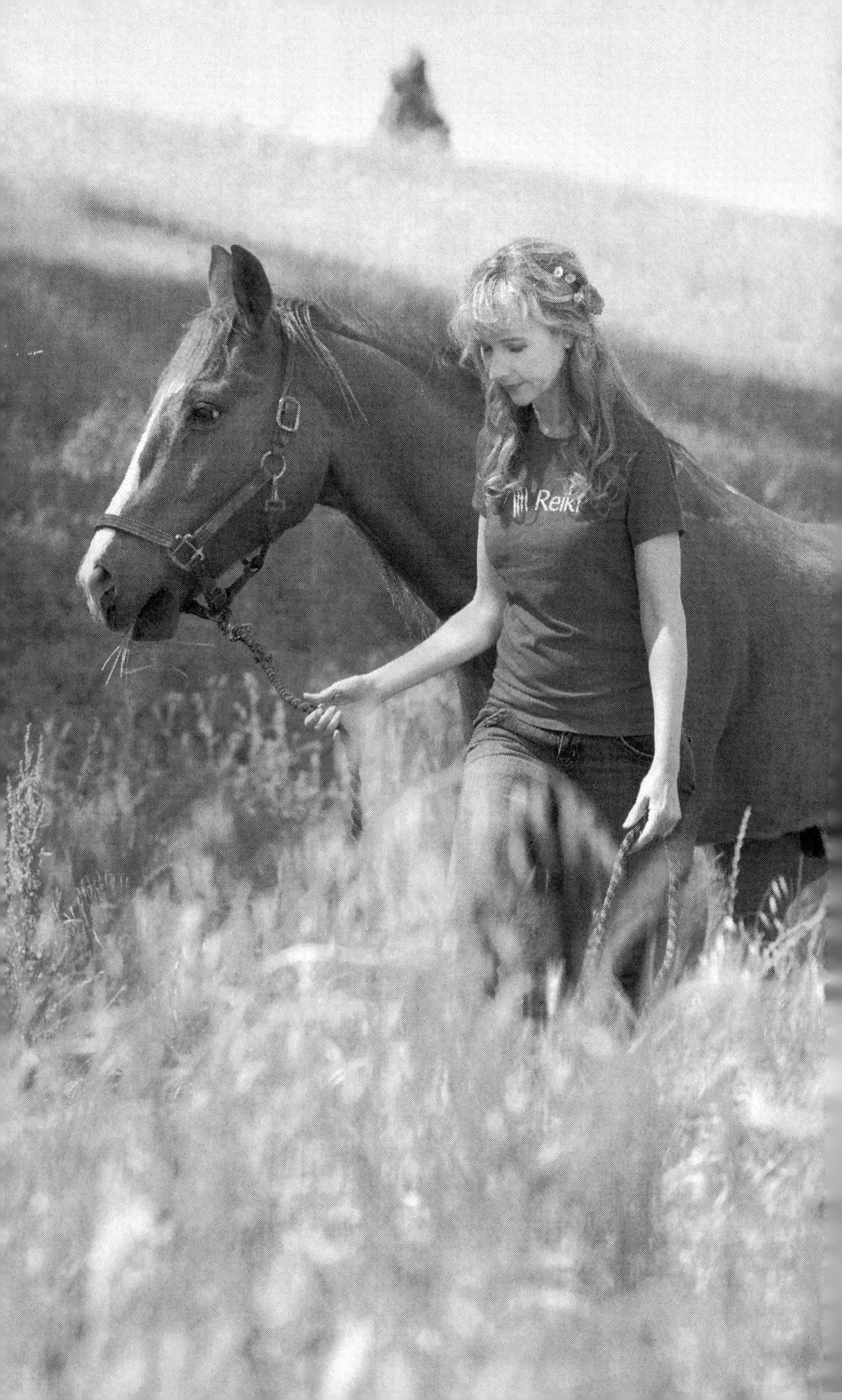
Reiki

## CHAPTER 2
# My Horse Teachers

*His hooves pound the beat, your heart sings the song.*

—Jerry Shulman

I CAN STILL REMEMBER it vividly—looking out my bedroom window at the tender age of five and seeing my neighbors across the street unloading their horse trailer, right on our own suburban Napa street! I ran outside and across the street in time to see a chestnut quarter horse walking across the sidewalk and onto their front lawn. Already I was completely enthralled. The neighbors called to me, "Hey, Kathleen, come over and meet our horse!" I gladly did so, sitting next to them on the lawn.

I will never forget the way the horse lowered his nose to greet me, letting me pet his head. It was at that moment that my heart suddenly belonged to the horse. Not really that particular horse, although he was quite charming, but a spark was struck within me for horses in general—wild horses, domesticated horses, confident horses, fearful horses, pampered horses, horses rescued from abuse and neglect. When that chestnut gelding touched his nose to my hand, my heart turned over and opened up, and I was never the same again.

From that moment on, everything in my childhood revolved around horses: imagining that I was riding a horse, imagining that I *was* a horse; collecting model horses to create herd families and enact horse "soap opera" adventures for hours, day after day, especially in the summertime. What did I want for every birthday and Christmas? A model horse and a horse book. As I got older, I even got some "horse weekend" trainings for presents now and again. My family couldn't afford to own a horse, or even to lease one, but when I was in middle school I began to take riding lessons, and this was a dream come true. I could only afford to ride a couple of times a month, but every day in between I would imagine myself on horseback and practice in my mind all the things I had learned in my lesson. My teacher would always be amazed the next time I rode, saying, "Hey, have you practiced this? You look like you've been riding!" I always smiled and said, "Yes, in my dreams, I ride every day!"

When I went away to college, horses disappeared from my life as I buried myself in my studies. Then I went to graduate school and become a teacher in an inner city community, and my connections to the country, to open space, and to horses became a distant memory.

### *Superstar Sonny, who brought me back to horses*

When I met Sonny, I hadn't been on a horse in many years. My sister had moved to the east Bay, about forty-five minutes away, and had begun riding a horse named Sonny in the Oakland hills. Oakland and horses, this was a revelation! A beautiful bay Arab in his early twenties, Sonny belonged to a friend of my sister's, who was looking for a sponsor for him. She had been with Sonny for over ten years, and when we were first introduced she told me, "This horse saved my life." She recounted to me how the sudden death of a close friend had pitched her into a powerful depression. Then she had found Sonny, and riding every day through beautiful open spaces—on trails that ran through meadows, hills, and forests—she had rediscovered her strength, remembered her joy, and healed her spirit. Now she had a new job, and she was unable to ride Sonny every day as he loved to do, and so was looking for someone to share this time with him. She didn't trust just anyone to ride Sonny, but since she was a good friend of my sister, she decided we could try it and see what he thought of me. "He's not that comfortable with everyone; he's very sensitive," she told me. "Mostly I ride bareback with a hackamore," she said. Well, this was all a bit new to me, but I thought, let's try it and see what happens.

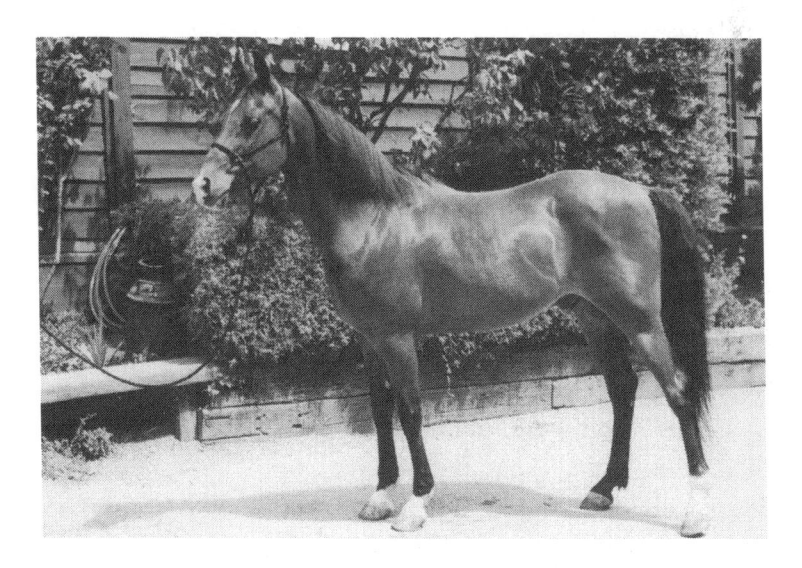

I grabbed Sonny's mane and pulled myself onto his bare back and asked him to walk around the arena, with just a halter and lead rope on his head. As soon as I felt my legs hanging down astride him, it was as if I had known him for many years. I closed my eyes, let my hands rest on his shoulders, and felt my hips sway with his steps. Oh, it felt so good, so right, to be riding again! After a few times around the arena, I opened my eyes finally and asked him to trot a bit. What a forward gait he had—and the smoothest trot I had ever felt! Even without a saddle and being completely rusty in my own balance, I had no trouble sitting the trot comfortably. I asked Sonny again to walk and he did so immediately, transitioning into a lovely forward walk, his ears pointed back toward me expectantly. Through this whole experience, my sister's friend watched quietly. Finally, she said, "Well, I've never seen him take to someone like this. Seems like you two are already friends!" In truth, I had tears of joy in my eyes, feeling Sonny under me. I absolutely couldn't wait to take him out on the trails!

Over the next few years, with my dog Dakota galloping at our side, Sonny and I navigated many beautiful trails in the Oakland hills. From redwood groves with forget-me-nots and ferns to sunny ridge trails with views spanning the whole San Francisco skyline, he took me wherever he wanted to go. Sonny knew those trails like the back of his hoof. I, on the other hand, had no idea where we were going. Knowing this, I told Sonny it was all up to him. Sometimes he chose trails that were longer, other times shorter. Sometimes we rode steep and fast, with lots of cantering, other times long and flat, with his wonderful smooth trot. When we'd meet hikers on the trail, inevitably Sonny would put his tail straight in the air, his head up, and lift up his feet into his amazing fancy trot, causing onlookers to gasp and point and smile. He also loved to stop and let children pet him.

Nothing spooked this horse. Nothing. A snake on the trail? Give it a wide berth and keep going. A log blocking the trail? Jump it. Crazy mountain bikers going too fast on the trail? So what! Once, we were going up a steep trail with a cliff on one side and a high hillside on the other when a lone bicyclist came tearing down the trail at about twenty-five miles per hour. By the time he skidded around the blind corner and saw us, there was nowhere for him to go. He slammed on the brakes and his back tire came up and flew sideways through the air, smacking Sonny on the hind end. What did Sonny do? He turned his ear towards the cyclist and swished his tail as if to say, "Whippersnapper!"

Another time we were riding at sunset and a rainstorm started. We trotted through the trees and the wind suddenly picked up, and branches and leaves from the eucalyptus all around us began to fall. Sonny barely twitched an ear, however, he did turn around and decide to cut our trail ride short that day. All the trails led back in a circle sooner or later so that we could find our way back to the barn, but I had no knowledge of the length of them. At every fork in the trail, Sonny would stop and ponder for a minute, as would I. Dakota, my dog, would sometimes choose for us, and Sonny would just follow him. Sometimes I would urge him one way or another, and he would agree. But most of the time, Sonny had in his mind exactly which way he wanted to go.

For a few wonderful years, I spent every Saturday morning with Sonny. Looking back on those experiences now that I have two horses of my own, I can hardly believe what an amazing horse Sonny was—how safe, how experienced, how wise. He took care of me on every trail, no matter what. He was patient with my novice nature. As a rider, those years with Sonny gave me a rock-solid seat, a light hand, and a certain trust in the horse that I suppose many humans may have never experienced. Sonny showed me in a very profound way how horses can be our teachers.

At that time in my life, I had also recently learned Reiki. Reiki was at that time a relatively unknown phenomenon in the U.S., and after my dog Dakota showed me that he loved to share Reiki, I wondered what Sonny would think of it. The first time I tried to share Reiki with him was in his stall as he ate his dinner. He stopped eating and stood still, very focused and interested, soaking it up. About halfway through the session, his whole body began to shake violently for about thirty seconds. Then he relaxed, but slowly raised his hind leg and held it in the air. After a few minutes he lowered it to the ground, but propped it a bit on the edge of his hoof. When I finished the session, I petted him all over his body and looked more closely at his leg. I could see the faint marks of old scars there; I hadn't ever noticed them before. On asking his person later, I learned that before Sonny was hers, he had lived on a big property and had once gotten caught up in some barbed wire. He hadn't been found for about twenty-four hours, and had been forced to stand on three legs for some time. The scars we could see with our eyes were from this incident, however I was sure that it was the scars we couldn't see that had been reached by Reiki. Perhaps some of that old trauma had been released by his shaking episode during the session. I often don't know exactly what Reiki is healing, but I know it always does something amazing!

From then on, each Saturday I would take Sonny out on the trails and afterwards share Reiki with him in his stall while he relaxed. What a wonderful time of bonding, of learning to speak the language of energy, of connecting to horse energy more deeply than I had ever done before. Sometimes Sonny wanted hands-on Reiki, sometimes he preferred hands-off. Sometimes he wanted a long session, other times a short one. Sometimes he slept, sometimes he ate, and sometimes he stood and looked at me. Every session was different. Sonny taught me how to be flexible and listen when sharing Reiki. He taught me that Reiki sessions can be done while standing or even walking. During this time, I noticed that even though he had some arthritis, Reiki eased his pain on days he was stiff, gave him peacefulness, and helped his mobility.

Eventually Sonny retired and moved to live far away, and I heard through the grapevine that he passed away. But I often think of him and our amazing trail rides, and I am so thankful for every moment we had together. My heart will always be full of gratitude for Sonny!

## *Leaning on Kodiak*

I have detailed Shawnee's story in the introduction to this book, but my other horse, Kodiak, has been a big part of my healing journey as well.

In 2011, I was diagnosed with breast cancer, and I underwent surgery that summer. Unfortunately, one side effect of the surgery was chronic pain and an inability to move my left arm. After several weeks of healing and physical therapy I was still very weak, but I knew I wanted to get back into the saddle as soon as possible! Astride a horse is my healing place.

I still remember the first time I rode after surgery. I felt so weak and fragile as I lifted myself, slowly and with one arm, into the saddle. I only walked around on Kodiak that day, but as soon as I could feel him moving beneath me, I had a memory

Heart To Heart With Horses | 25

of strength within me. I knew I could get better! It's funny how just that familiar feeling of being in the saddle was able to help me remember my strong spirit. Without the ability to use my left arm, I had to depend wholly on my seat and legs while riding, so I can honestly say that I became a much better rider due to my physical problems. Might as well make lemonade out of lemons!

Having Kodiak take care of me was a wonderful experience. Before this time in my life, I thought I had always been the one to take care of him and offer healing support, sharing Reiki for small cuts and scrapes or an abscess or stone bruise on his hoof. What a gift that he let me lean on him as I recovered! As a result of being so weak, I lost a great deal of confidence in my riding skills. Sometimes I would think about what would happen if I fell off onto my injured arm or onto my chest. I stopped riding outside the arena and became very timid about riding when there was rain or wind, or anything that might spook a horse. Sometimes I would spend time riding Kodiak at a walk in the arena, chanting Reiki mantras for my own healing. This was the first time that it occurred to me that it might be possible to share Reiki while riding!

Kodiak seemed to enjoy the sound of my voice and the chants, keeping his ears on me the whole time. Each time I rode, he was always calm and centered; he never spooked or made a sudden movement. My confidence slowly returned, and I began to venture out of the arena and feel brave enough to ride without chanting. It was as if Kodiak was demonstrating how to be brave, so that I would remember my own courage. I could feel he was taking care of me, and soon I practiced going a bit faster. After being laid up for so long, once I could be brave enough to trot and canter with the wind blowing on my face again, I felt so free!

Looking back on this experience, I realize that what Kodiak was doing for me is very similar to what I have done for other horses through sharing meditation. When we can model a Reiki way of being in the world, it can help those around us to remember their own inner strength. Just as I have modeled peacefulness for so many fearful horses over the years, letting them choose their own time to come forward and connect for healing, Kodiak was completely peaceful in the face of my own fears, patiently waiting until I got back my riding confidence.

I wanted to share this story about my experience with Kodiak because sometimes we feel that we have to be "perfect" in order to share anything beautiful with our horses. But the reality is that even if we have physical and emotional struggles, we already *are* perfect in our heart and spirit. When we go through tough times, we just have to dig a bit deeper to remember how bright our inner light is. Doing so will help us to get through life's challenges.

I am so grateful to the horses in my life who have taught me so much about heart to heart connection and compassion between species. Besides modeling the deepest compassionate virtues of Reiki practice, horses have always accepted me as I am, somehow always seeing beyond my limitations into my True Self. Through their patience, kindness and healing presence they have helped bring out my inner strength and spiritual gifts, and being with them has brought the joy and wonder of my inner child back into my adult life. My horses don't have to "practice" the system of Reiki, because they effortlessly *live* Reiki, inspiring me to do the same!

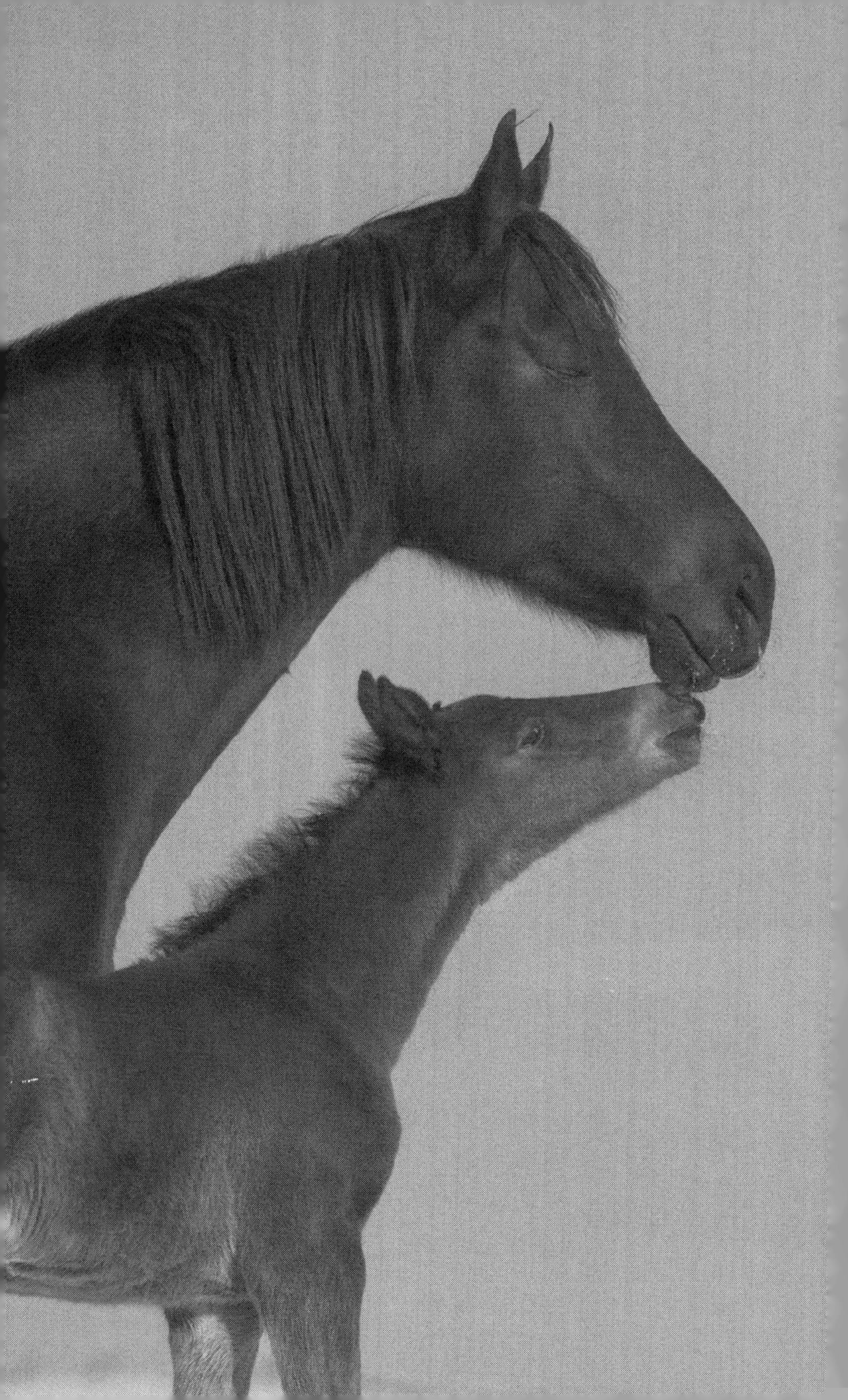

## CHAPTER 3
# Peace + Love = Healing

*Let your love flow outward through the universe,*
*To its height, its depth, its broad extent,*
*A limitless love, without hatred or enmity.*
*Then as you stand or walk,*
*Sit or lie down,*
*As long as you are awake,*
*Strive for this with a one-pointed mind;*
*Your life will bring heaven to earth.*

—Sutta Nipata

SHARING OUR LIFE with horses, caring for them, getting to know each other, and in so doing transcending the differences between species to create lasting bonds and lifelong relationships—these are some of the gifts that our love for horses can bring to our lives. Rescuing horses, advocating for them, loving them, being a voice for the powerless and for good are acts that not only help horses but also shine compassion out into the world.

All of these are things that all horse lovers already do, and in my experience, adding Reiki to the mix can help us to do even more, or, I should say, *be* even more. Each moment with our horses is an opportunity to create peace and love. Being peace and love with our horses will help us to understand and experience true healing.

This may sound easy, to simply be peace and love, but in practice, it can be quite difficult. We so often find ourselves in a place of worry, anger, fear, and distraction. Even though we love our horses, our inner emotional state might be very out of balance, scattered, or in disharmony, and this can detract from our ability to connect with them. Or we may find our horses going through difficulties of body, mind, or spirit, and if we are very stressed out by this, we will find it very difficult to help them get better.

Reiki gives us the tools to transform ourselves and our horses with peace and love, so that each day with our horses can become a healing miracle. When peace and love thrive, suffering and sadness lose their power. In sharing Reiki with our horses, we learn to share peace and love, even in difficult times. Reiki techniques teach us to hold this peaceful, powerful state of mind within our own energy. Our horses will sense this energetic balance and be drawn to it, and can find strength and balance to heal themselves. In fact, this space of peace and love is what healing is all about. I believe that when we connect with our horses heart to heart, all things are possible!

The following two case studies illustrate the ability of Reiki to embrace even the most challenging situations with peace and love, thus harnessing the infinite power of healing potential! Let Reiki help you widen your radiance of peace and love, so that healing can transform your life and the lives of the horses you love.

# Case Study: *Recipe for Healing: Love and Reiki*
# by Susi Canter

The owners of Ronnie, a twenty-four-year-old thoroughbred horse, were feeling the effects of the economy, and I knew that keeping Ronnie boarded at my stable was becoming a burden on them. I also knew that Ronnie was sick, and might not live much longer. I asked the owners to sell Ronnie to me for a dollar, which they did. My husband and I felt that she might not live long, but that we could make her remaining time comfortable. The vet had told me that he was sure Ronnie had Cushing's disease, and had her owners asked to have her put down, he would have agreed. Knowing this vet to be someone who would not willingly put any animal to sleep, I knew he did not hold out much hope for her.

One Christmas Eve, Ronnie lay down in the pasture, breathing heavily. I shocked my boarders by lying close to her head (although I do not recommend this, for safety reasons) and sharing Reiki with her. Her eyes were dull and empty, but after a short Reiki session, she got up and walked to her stall. That was the first of many evenings I spent sitting in Ronnie's stall with her, sharing Reiki. I was sure my boarders thought that I had finally gone nuts! Yet I knew Ronnie needed me, and I decided being thought of as nuts might not be such a bad thing.

In our second session, Ronnie rewarded my efforts by placing her head in my hands for a long time. Tears poured down my face. The next evening, although severely lame, she stumbled toward me for our session. This time, she put her face down and looked right at me, and I was amazed to see that the dead look was gone from her eyes! Each time I stood with her, I would visualize her running happily through pastures. I also told her that I loved her, and those three little words gave the spiritual energy between us a wonderful boost which both of us felt. I was rewarded again by Ronnie placing her head in my hands. Once the horse in the next stall even stretched toward me to put her head on my shoulder. The vet could not believe the difference in Ronnie, and asked what I had done. I told him: love and Reiki!

Five months later, Ronnie is on a special diet with supplements, and we share Reiki three times a week. She has come through the pain of being severely lame, and while she will never be ridden again, she has thrilled everyone at the barn, now that she is able to trot happily around her pasture. Ronnie taught me not to be afraid of sharing Reiki, even if the humans around me might not understand what I am doing. She also taught me that the words "I love you" can reach an animal's soul and heal with a tremendous power. My experience with Ronnie has shown me that there is no greater passion for me than sharing Reiki, and no greater gratitude in my heart than for being able to assist animals in healing themselves.

## Case Study: *Reiki and Barkkis*
## by Jutta Rannanmäki

Barkkis, a purebred Tersk horse, was born twenty years ago on a stud farm in Russia. She grew up in a herd in the mountain district of Caucasus, and came to Finland at the age of four. During her life, she has been involved in all kinds of exercises: dressage, show jumping, and endurance riding. She found her current family seven years ago. The whole family was taking riding lessons at a riding school, and at one weekend camp the mother fell in love with this beautiful white horse, who had the most wonderful nature. Both parents felt she would be a perfect horse for their young daughters as well. It was clear at once that they would take her home with them.

Barkkis turned out to be a very wise horse. She carefully considers everything she does, looks where she puts her feet, and doesn't jump around. I guess that is the reason why she has always been the leader in any herd. She never had any special problems with her health, until one day she started limping on her left front leg. It was not a small injury; she truly was a three-legged horse. She was brought to the vet many times, and received many different diagnoses: navicular disease, foot joint arthritis, and bone spavin. She got cortisone shots to the hoof twice, and also a Tildren shot. As a last resort the vet tried shockwave treatments to the hoof four times, but nothing made the situation better. The staff at the clinic didn't hold out much hope, as they were out of potential treatments.

Barkkis kept on limping, and bit by bit the family started to lose their faith. They didn't want to give up, because Barkkis was so dear to them, so they brought her to a nearby stable to try to rehabilitate her. Walking was one thing Barkkis was able to do, so that was what they did, as much as her health would allow. I became involved in their lives about five months later, when we met at the stables. We talked for a while about Barkkis's situation and about Reiki, which was a new subject to them. We decided I should share Reiki with Barkkis whenever I had the time.

The first signs that Barkkis's healing process had begun came a week or two after we began our Reiki sessions. Her limping lessened, and she was so full of energy that she started bucking from joy. Even the father of the family, who had doubted Reiki's ability to help at first, came home one day from the stables and said that he had seen a new look in Barkkis's eyes—as if she were telling him that she hadn't given up, and so he couldn't give up on her either.

In the three months since our first session. Barkkis and I continue to share two to three Reiki sessions every week. Her spirit is amazingly cheered up, and it is as if she is a totally new horse—young again, with no signs of pain. The only thing she wants to do is gallop; trotting and walking are too slow for her. We are all living in gratitude for each additional day with Barkkis. I guess Barkkis herself is most grateful for the special family she has, the family who understood her needs and gave her time to heal, supporting her recovery all the way.

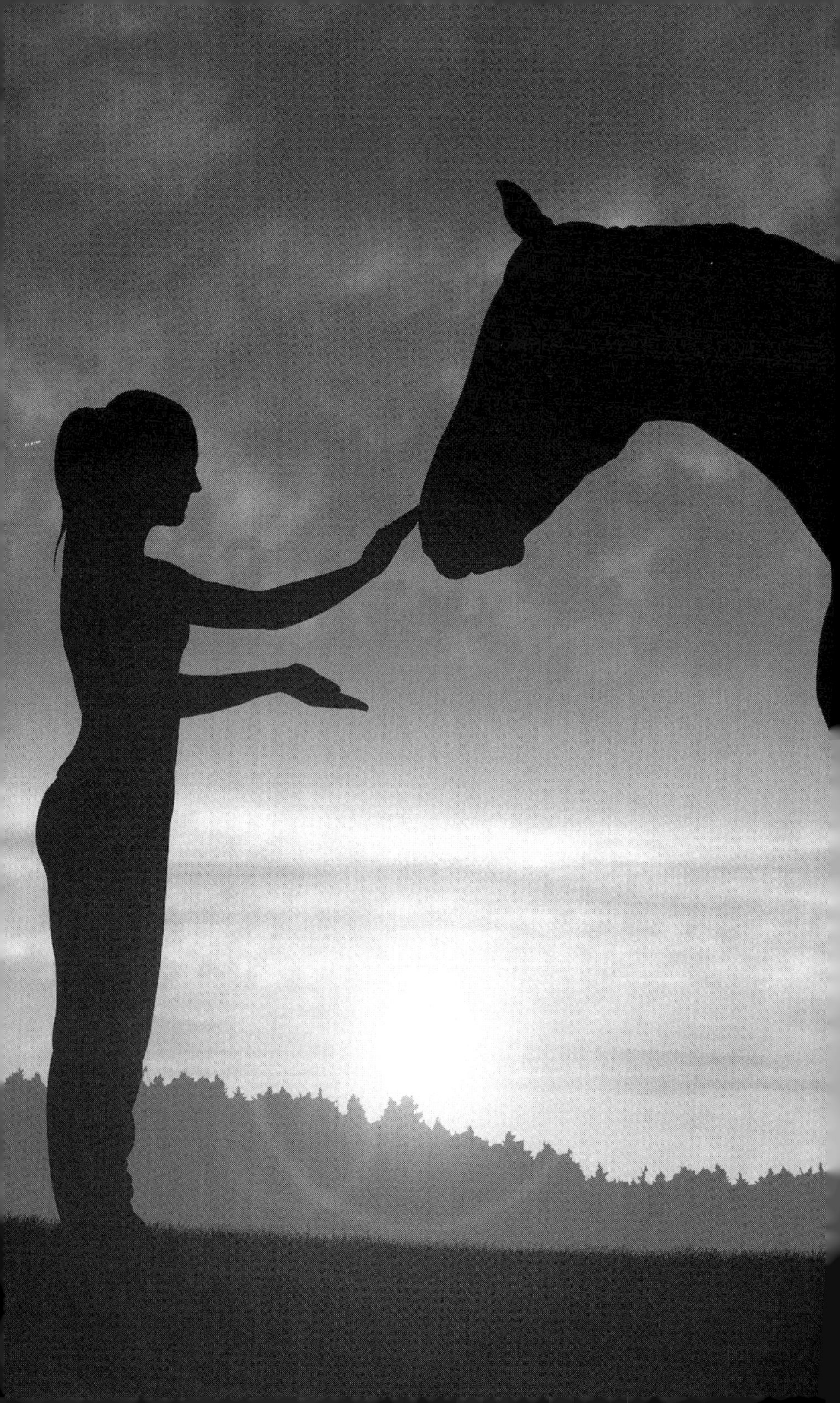

# CHAPTER 4
## Healing from Within

*"Peace comes from within. Do not seek it without."*

—Buddha

THIS QUOTE FOR me sums up the importance of our inner work and our inner healing; it reminds us of why it is essential that we remember our inner essence, power, and strength. Once we access this strength, we can truly be Reiki and help our horses no matter what they're going through—yes, even through the process of transitioning out of their earthly bodies. We can do it.

The first question then becomes: how do we find this peace and this healing within ourselves? The number one means for me is *being*, not doing. Meditation is the best way I know to let go of doing and remember how to simply be.

In reality, this is all we are doing when we connect to horses using the practices of Reiki: we are learning how to be with them in a mindful, present, and compassionate way. This mindful presence is what creates the healing. Reiki techniques help us learn how to create a healing space—a space that is simply peace from within ourselves—and learn how to radiate that space outward.

When we do so, our horses are able to connect with us for whatever they're open to receiving or whatever they need.

The famous Japanese Buddhist teacher Dogen said, "Take a backward step and study the self thoroughly. When we study the self thoroughly, we understand others thoroughly as well. As a result, self and other merge in a single vastness. Self and other, saving the self and saving all sentient beings, are a single reality." When I first read that quote, it reminded me of the system of Reiki, and how although we may get into the practice of Reiki to help horses, it really starts within ourselves first. Reiki also nurtures connection, and often when we are sharing Reiki with our horses we can feel a merging into oneness, where species differences melt away. So in one way, because we are all One, we can see that in healing ourselves, we're taking the first step towards healing others. On our own, it may take many years to even begin to touch upon the profound nature of this kind of connection, but with the help of our horses, who are so sensitive and such great teachers, we may begin to have small experiences of this connection immediately.

This is why I recommend meditating with your horses. Stand with them in the pasture and see how they respond by relaxing, connecting, and healing. Also, see how you yourself respond. You may find that your meditation goes much deeper. It might be easier for you to relax your mind. You might feel the strength of the meditation much more quickly than when you practice alone. You might surprise yourself at how long you can stay focused!

I remember a very flighty, nervous mare that I worked with years ago. She wouldn't stand still for anyone. It was so interesting to see how she responded to people even just walking by her stall. When her person asked me to share Reiki with her, I wondered how it would go. This was in the early days of my practice, but still I had an intuitive sense that my own sense of peace and calm would be vital if I was to hope for any kind of connection with the mare.

Before I entered the stall, I spent several minutes practicing Reiki *hara* breathing, so that my own energy would be very calm. My intention was to simply be with the mare in a peaceful state of mind, and invite her to join me there. Amazingly, she was immediately responsive, and within minutes showed signs of relaxation such as licking and chewing. Her person stood by wide-eyed, wondering how in the world her flighty, anxious horse was able to relax into a nap with a stranger within five minutes!

It seems such a simple thing, to relax, and yet this experience really opened up my eyes to the power of peace, how it radiates out to others from within our spirits. Inner focus, mindfulness, and presence: they are so simple, and yet so powerful! Horses always show us that healing starts from within—they are so sensitive, they will show us when we are in the right state of mind. But healing is also about a partnership, and we help each other along the way. When we connect, compassion grows on both sides.

Those of you reading this may have picked up this book thinking, "Well, I want to help the horses in my life." But you very soon may find yourself saying, "What happened? I think I got healed, too. What a surprise!" This is another of the gifts of Reiki—the healing partnership that develops between you and the horses you connect with. The more we learn to go inward, to let go and to *be* rather than *do*, the more we open ourselves up to infinite possibility and to the unexpected. There are many things that can happen within the Reiki Space.

Of the importance of consciousness in the state of our world, Eckhart Tolle has said, "No matter how active we are, how much effort we make, our state of consciousness creates our world, and if there is no change on that inner level, no amount of action will make any difference." I love that quotation. When we know ourselves and remember our true nature, focusing on connection, compassion, wisdom, courage, hope, and so on, only then can we create, hold, and radiate the special atmosphere of peace that will change not only our inner world and who we are, but also our outer world and the horses we come in contact with.

How do we find our center, so that we can radiate this peace? First, we must learn to be present with ourselves. Meditation will help us, so we mustn't neglect our spiritual practice. Make time each day to meditate, even when you are busy. In fact, the busier you are, the more vital it is to meditate! You just might find that when you do, because you're more peaceful and centered, you have the energy to do more in your life.

The more often you practice, the longer the centering effects of meditation last, even when you're not meditating. There's a resonance and vibration that just keeps going and going and going, long after you get up and resume your daily activities. And this lasting resonance gets stronger and longer the more you practice. In fact the real power of meditation is this inner peace that resonates throughout the day. It's the most important result of our meditation practice: to help us bring this peaceful presence beyond the meditation cushion into each moment of our lives.

When we practice, we are building our meditation muscles. It's good to practice all the time, not just when you're feeling at your best. Sometimes we might say, "Oh, I'm feeling great today! I'm in a really good space, and the weather is really nice and all is well, so I'm going to sit and do my meditation." That's all very well and good, but believe it or not, when you're *not* feeling well might be the best time for you to sit down and do your practice. It is at those difficult moments—for example, when you're sick, and you can't run away from it even if you want to—that you have to remember to just *be*, because you have to surrender your body to quiet and rest in order to heal. So at these times we can say to ourselves, "All right—I'm here in this moment; I'm just going to relax and surrender to it."

You will find that even if you begin your meditation stressed out or not feeling very well, your mind focused on other things, if you just stick with the practice, things will get better. Your distracted feeling will soon dissipate into a space of peace that you create through your meditation. That peace starts with the light in your inner core, and then begins to get stronger and stronger and radiate outward. At some point during your meditation you may even realize that you had that feeling of peace the whole time—you just needed to access it. Then you realize that even when you are sick, weak, or not feeling well, your inner peace, your inner light, your True Self is always there. It helps to be practicing meditation all the time, so when you're not feeling your best physically, your spiritual memory can take over. It's so good for us to meditate, to let go of our thoughts, to rest in a quiet, peaceful place. It's good for us and it's good for our horses.

There's another quote that I love, also by Eckhart Tolle, "You are never more essentially, more deeply yourself than when you are still. When you are still, you are who you were before you temporarily assumed this physical and mental form called a person. You are also who you will be when the form dissolves. When you are still, you are who you are beyond your temporal existence, consciousness—unconditioned, formless, eternal."

How does this inner stillness affect our horses? It can give us the foundation of peace and balance to be able to be present with them in their times of health challenges, for whatever that looks like—good, bad, joy, suffering, all of it. When they look to us for comfort and support, we will be there, without faltering.

Of course it's not always easy, because we love our horses so much! We might feel that love even if they're not our own horses. For example, we might be very connected to and empathize strongly with horses we're working with in sanctuaries. Sometimes our emotions make it very difficult to create that space of peace and hold it and radiate it outward. But that's what we need to do because that is what helps them so much.

There are several things to remember so that you can radiate stillness and peacefulness for a horse with whom you're sharing Reiki.

### *Remember your grounding.*

The founder of aikido, Morihei Ueshiba, said in his book *The Art of Peace*: "Every sturdy tree that towers over human beings owes its existence to a deeply rooted core." We want to be like a tree with those roots. We've got to keep growing upward and outward to be able to help our horses more and more. But to grow upward and outward we have to always be nurturing our roots. Our roots, in turn, nurture our inner core. So remember your grounding.

When we peel back the layers and heal ourselves, we find our center, and in that center, we discover we are stable. We are grounded. We have a strong foundation that nothing can shake. When we discover this, it becomes easier to clear our energy river of blockages, attachments, judgments, expectations, and ego. Let go, let go, let go, and in so doing, you will go deeper and deeper into the energy of healing for yourself. The freer you are with your own energy, the more easily it radiates out from your center, stronger and stronger and stronger, without effort. It's just the nature of it.

Buddhist teacher Hongzhi Zhengjue said: "You must take a backward step and directly reach the middle of the circle from where light issues forth."

It's good to think of our practice in that way: that we have to step backward to reach the middle of the circle of light. We always think of stepping forward and *doing*. Instead, let's step backward and *be*. And what do we find when we're present, still and grounded? We find our light, our True Self. When we stand in our light, we cannot be knocked over by emotions. When we see the light within ourselves, it becomes possible to see it in others. Compassion will easily manifest within this beautiful light. Pity cannot exist in the light of compassion. Pity is an unhelpful emotion, that like worry or anger, makes it difficult (if not impossible) to support our horses when they are facing difficulty. Find your inner light, and shine bright to help your horses find their way back into balance.

### *Realize your true strength.*

Something else to remember that will really help the horses with whom you share Reiki is to remember your power, which resides in your spirit, in your inner light, in your True Self. All the strength you ever need is already within you. When we talk about inner strength, we have to ask the question, "What does it mean to be strong?" So often we might think that it is only when our bodies are strong and we can do a lot of things. We might think at first that when we are sick or have an illness and can only lie in bed, it means that we are weak.

We need to shift our thinking about strength. My own personal experience with physical illness has been actually the opposite of what I might once have thought; when I found that I was unable to do, unable to go around in my physical body feeling great and doing lots of actions outwardly in my life, it forced me to go inward, to let go of my body in a different way than I had before. So I spent more time in meditation, more time in contemplation, and guess what? I found inspiration. I learned to dissolve my sadness and worry and stress in that peaceful space that radiated from my core. I couldn't ignore it by busying myself with lots of physical or mental distractions. All I could do was surrender to it: be still with it all, and then, amazingly, I could feel my suffering dissolving away into peace. This feeling would even stay with me for some time after my meditation was over.

Once you learn to be peace and strength for yourself, you will know beyond a shadow of a doubt you can be there for your horses. You can hold that space for them and they can step into it and be healed, release their fear, sadness, and suffering. It is as if you are a mirror, reflecting back to your horse his own inner strength. You will then realize that even in the most challenging circumstance there is always light and always hope. As Ralph Waldo Emerson said, "When it's dark enough, you can see the stars."

### *Nurture yourself.*

Caregiver burnout and fatigue results from too much physical action without concern for the nurturing of our inner spirits. Without our spiritual practice to help us remember, we can forget our inner light and lose our way.

The more grounded and strong we become within ourselves, the more energy we have to do good for others. In addition, we will see bigger and better responses from the horses with whom we connect. No problem is too big to be solved, no issue unable to be healed. Meditation helps us step into the natural flow of the universe. This is something that the great spiritual teacher John Daido Loori reminds us of: "When we step out of the way, our life pours through us. The universe pours through us."

That's a funny thing, isn't it: to realize that by going inward, we will actually affect greater change on the outside. I would love for you to hold that realization in your heart and mind as you contemplate ways to help the horses in your life. The following meditation may help you reconnect to your inner strength when you're feeling burned out.

## Case Study: *Lady Learns to Trust*
## by Cindie Ambar

I first met Lady in December of 2011. She had been described as "explosive," bolting at every attempt at human contact. On my first visit to see Lady and her mother, Snowflakes, Lady was very curious about me. I could feel her wanting to connect, but she stopped herself each time she crept more than a few feet in my direction. I had intentionally placed myself about ten feet away from her for my Reiki meditation and just held a loving space, giving her the option to come to me if and when she was ready. There were no obvious signs Lady was connecting with me, but I trusted the healing was beginning.

On my second visit, both Lady and Snowflakes approached me and nickered as I opened the gate. Lady stayed close to me the entire time, sniffing my face and body for long intervals, nibbling at and licking my hands, but ran if I made the slightest movement in her direction. Snowflakes, who had been hesitant during my first visit, moved closer to me, dropped her head, and became deep in relaxation.

This same pattern continued for my third and fourth visits, with Lady more at peace each time and less likely to take off running when there was movement on my part. At this point, I was able to touch her very lightly.

The day of my fifth visit, a major transition took place. I had been meditating with the horses for almost twenty minutes when Lady started to close her eyes. This meant that I had established a great deal of trust with her, and she felt safe enough to let down her guard. She continued with her eyes closed for few moments, starting to drop into sleep. She paused and let out a couple of little groans. I then observed some very, very deep breathing, as well as a period in which she was breathing very shallowly and quickly, as if she was processing—moving something through. She slept (standing up) for about half an hour, occasionally opening her eyes, stretching, and closing them to go back to sleep.

After this visit, Lady opened up and I was able to touch and connect with her more. On the following visit Snowflakes also let down her guard and allowed me to get very close. I felt a deep heart connection to them. Two months later, when I was working with Lady and Snowflakes, the unexpected happened: Lady approached me and placed her chest close to my chest and her head on my shoulder. We stood there together in a loving space for a very long time. What an honor to watch her healing unfold!

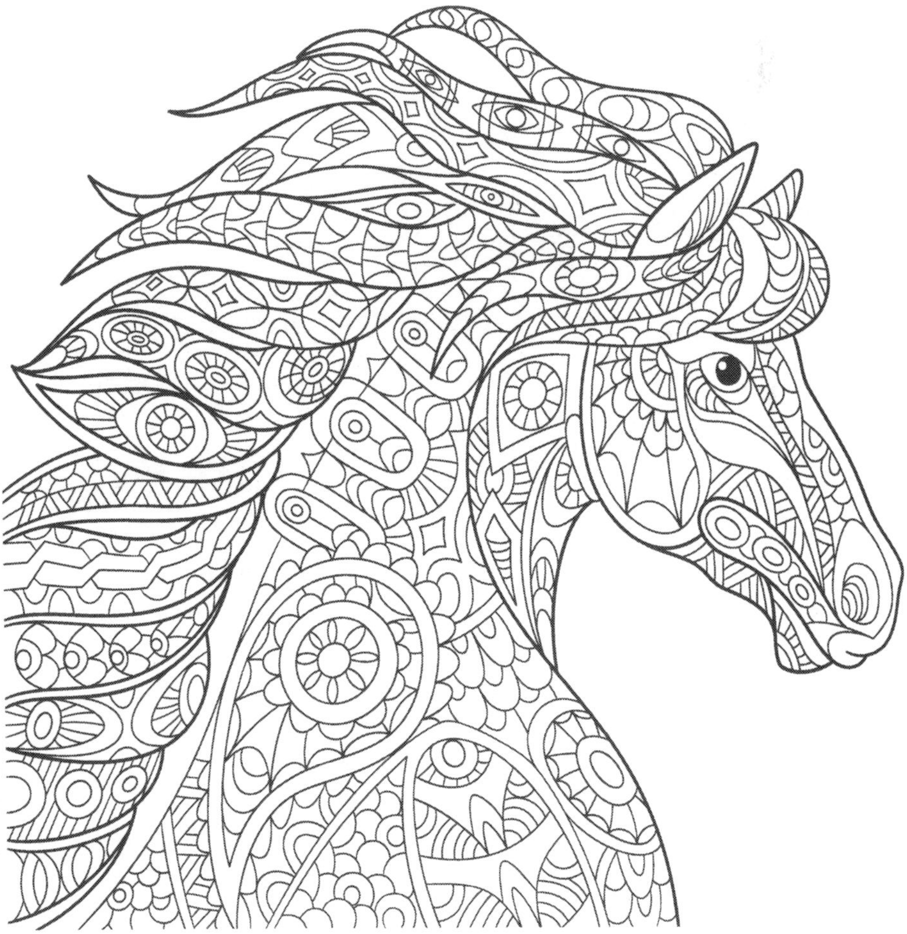

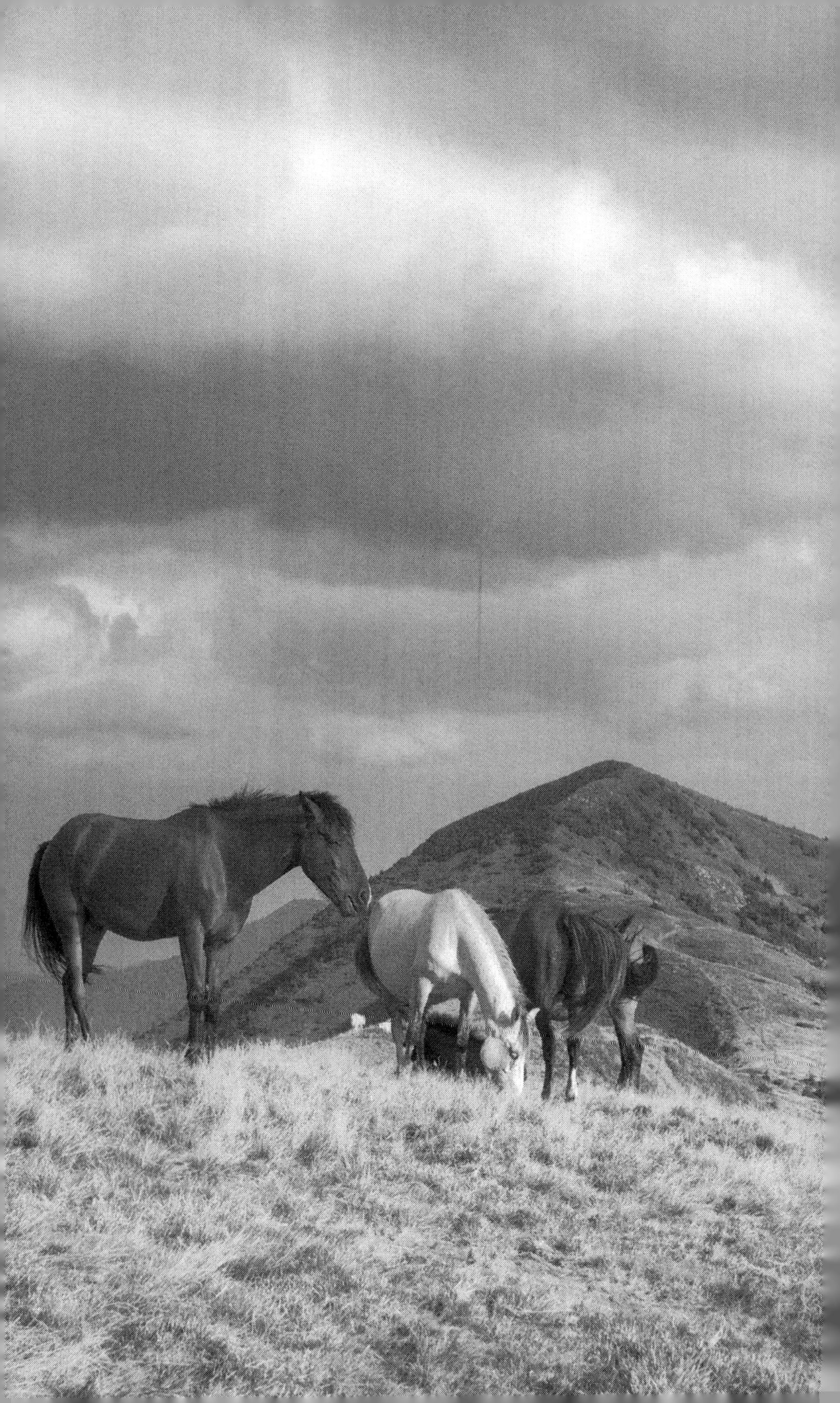

## Rainbow Healing Meditation

Find a comfortable position in which to sit. Make sure your spine is nice and straight, your shoulders are relaxed back, and your arms are relaxed. Rest your hands palms up or palms down on your lap, whatever is most comfortable. Close your eyes and take a nice, deep, cleansing breath and let it out slowly. Take another deep breath and let it out slowly.

As you breathe, feel yourself relaxing more and more with each breath, letting go of all the concerns of the day; just being present with your inhale and your exhale. Feel yourself totally present with your body in this moment.

For this meditation, I would like you to invite in a special horse in your life, or a few horses, or maybe a whole group of horses, like the wild horses of the world. Whatever horses come to your heart right now, I would like you to invite them to share in this meditation and healing space with you. Open your heart to them, and see them here with you right now.

Now visualize your body; see it composed of several layers of bright, vibrant rainbow colors. These layers begin at the surface of your skin, and each successive layer of beautiful color goes deeper and deeper and deeper into your being, to the very core of your inner essence. See your body as a beautiful rainbow. We are now going to travel through all of the layers of this beautiful rainbow body.

Let's start at the outermost layer—your skin. I would like you to visualize the color red. I would like you to focus on your roots reaching down into the earth. Just feel that connection to the earth, and see this beautiful layer of red glowing over the whole surface of your skin.

Within this beautiful layer of color I would like you to feel courage glowing and shining, feel the beautiful spiritual gift of

Heart To Heart With Horses | 47

courage inside of you that you always have access to. I would like you to see it here in this beautiful layer of red, in your being and in your connection to the earth. Feel the healing that exists in this beautiful red layer of courage. You *are* courage. Allow it to just wash over you, heal you, and strengthen you. Sit with this for a bit.

Now move more deeply into that beautiful layer of red. Just beneath it, you will find orange: a beautiful, vibrant, luminescent color. This inner layer surrounds your being, just inside the layer of red. If you like, you can now put your hands over your lower belly.

Feel, within this layer of beautiful orange color, your spiritual gift of joy and harmony. Feel this joy and harmony spreading within your whole being, permeating all of that beautiful orange layer that wraps itself around you. Feel the healing that exists within this beautiful orange layer. You are joy; you are harmony. Allow them to wash over you, heal you, and strengthen you. Sit with this for a bit.

Just beneath the beautiful orange layer, I would like you to see a lovely color of yellow all around your whole being. You're going deeper and deeper into your being. You can now put your hands over your solar plexus and just see that yellow color spreading throughout your whole being, touching the orange and the red.

I want you to feel this beautiful yellow color as your spiritual gifts of wisdom, expansion, and freedom of spirit. Feel those gifts flowing freely through this vibrant yellow color within your whole being, healing and strengthening you. With each color, we move closer and closer to the core of your spirit. Sit with this for a bit.

Let's visualize now another layer just inside the yellow; a beautiful layer of remarkable green color. Place your hands over your heart and see green spreading over your whole body.

Allow yourself to bask in that beautiful, vibrant green, and to feel open to your spiritual gifts of balance, love, and compassion. Feel these gifts flowing from this stunning green layer of light within your being; feel how easy it is to connect to healing and strengthening from these gifts. You are balance. You are love. You are compassion. Feel them wash over your being. Sit with this for a bit.

Now move even further into the layers of your being. Just inside the beautiful green layer, I would like you to see a glowing layer of blue light, a bright, luminous blue. Place your hands, palm over palm, just off your body in front of your throat.

See this luminous blue light radiating through your entire being, touching these other beautiful colors of green, yellow, orange, and red as we get closer and closer to your inner spirit. Allow yourself to feel open to your spiritual gifts of contentment and tranquility, feeling the energy of those gifts flowing strongly in the blue light. They spread healing and strength through your whole being. You are contentment. You are tranquility. Sit with this for a bit.

Now, moving even further, visualize a beautiful, deep, indigo color. You can place your hands, palm over palm, in front of your forehead. See this beautiful indigo color getting closer and closer to the inner core of your being and shining out vibrantly. Allow yourself to feel open to your spiritual gifts of truth and intuition. Feel the energy of those gifts flowing so beautifully within the indigo light, which is spreading within your whole being and touching upon all the other colors of the rainbow. Feel how you are healed and strengthened by the light. You are truth. You are intuition. Sit with this for a bit.

Moving even further into your spiritual core, I would like you to now visualize a beautiful layer of violet light touching the indigo light, and then spreading within your whole being. You

Heart To Heart With Horses | 49

can place your palms on top of your head. See this beautiful violet light shining, radiating outward. Open yourself to your spiritual gifts of awareness, spirit, and the beautiful energy that is your life force.

Feel these gifts flowing strongly through the violet light. Feel how healing it is for your whole being seeing the beautiful colors of the rainbow, violet, indigo, blue, green, yellow, orange, and red, all of the layers touching each other and radiating outward. You are awareness. You are spirit. You are life. Sit with this for a bit.

Now, moving to the deepest place in the core of your being and spirit, I would like you to visualize a core of vibrant, bright white light. This is the very core of your being.

Take your hands from your crown and open them, palms up, just above your head, allowing yourself to feel open to your spiritual gifts of purity, innocence, and peace. Feel those gifts flowing so strongly through this vibrant white light, which is so bright, at the very core of your being. The white touches the violet, touches the indigo, touches the blue, touches the green, the yellow, the orange, and the red, creating a beautiful rainbow radiating out from your whole body, radiating from your whole being out into the universe. You are healed and strengthened by these gifts. You are purity. You are innocence. You are peace. Sit with this for a bit.

Remember that we always have these beautiful colors, and also the gifts that go with them. We can choose to radiate into the universe the vibrations of courage, joy, wisdom, balance, contentment, truth, spirit, and peace. Feel all of this beautiful color and energy flowing through and expanding outward from your body and all around you, like a beautiful rainbow spreading wide into the universe. And now, simply invite the horses you love into this beautiful rainbow of healing: your horses, horses in your life, horses of the world. Bring them to your heart and mind and offer this beautiful rainbow space to them, to share with them for healing.

As you feel your beautiful rainbow light shining, remember that it is always there. This healing is always available to you and to the horses in your heart. All these spiritual gifts are inside you, just waiting to radiate out and shine into the world, to help horses. You just have to remember. This meditation will help you!

Now take a moment to thank the horses for their participation in the healing, for their connection, and then set your intention to finish the meditation. Bring your awareness back to your physical body. Put your hands over your lower belly and feel your grounding, your stability, and your center on the earth.

When you're ready, take a nice, deep, cleansing breath and slowly come back and open your eyes.

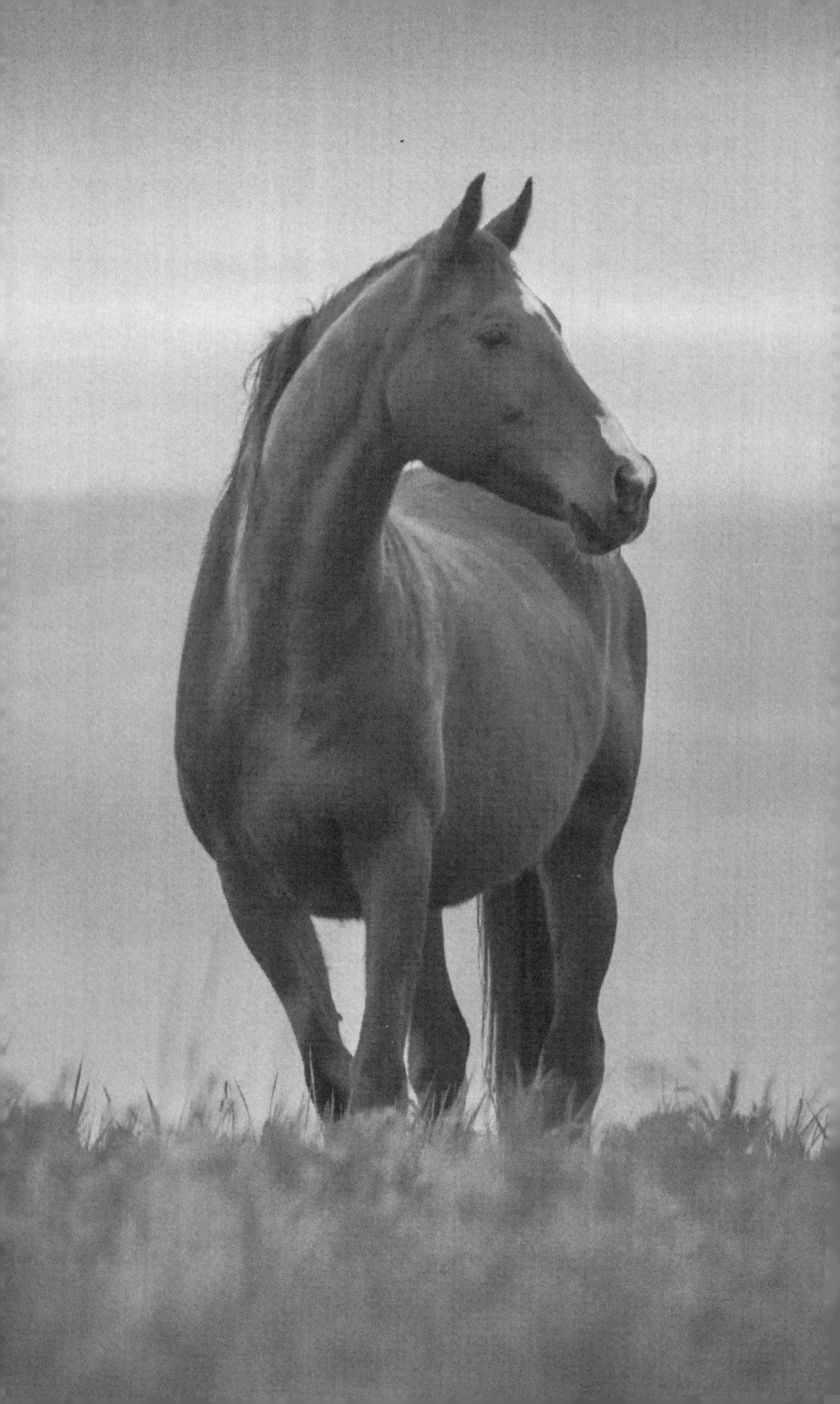

## CHAPTER 5
# Horses as Teachers

*"When we listen to our horses, we get an education. When we don't, we get experience."*

—Mark Rashid

HORSES INNATELY HELP us to open our hearts so that we can access the limitless love that resides there. For me, sharing Reiki with horses is not just about healing injuries, illness, or emotional issues. At its core, practicing Reiki meditation is a profound way to let love flow outward into the universe, not only for the horse we are with, but also for all the horses who need healing in the world.

Reiki helps us to remember that we are all one in this beautiful universe. As the love flows out, as we hold a compassionate, loving space for our horses, there is a beautiful, healing ripple effect out into the world, bringing the power of limitless love to all horses, and all beings. Energetically, our small acts of love resound very loudly into the universe.

So when you are connecting heart to heart with your wonderful horse, set your intention to share that beautiful heart space with all horses around the world. Why not spread the love? In this heart connection, the love flows both ways: as we are holding a loving space for the horses, they doing the same for us, while also teaching us powerful lessons about life and healing.

## *Teachers of meditation*

When we spend time with our horses in that natural quietness of their way of being, even if we're just in the pasture standing with them as they graze, our busy human minds can easily empty of everything. We feel much more at peace just being near them. In our day-to-day lives we might find ourselves sitting on our meditation cushion, trying so hard, saying to ourselves, "Okay, I'm trying to empty my mind, trying to get quiet and get close to the energy." But we might find it difficult to sit still, or frustrating because our minds are so active and distracted. When we're with a horse, we can find peacefulness effortlessly. We can quiet our minds easily. Time goes by and we hardly notice it. The feel of their manes in our fingers, the sound of their teeth pulling up grass, the earth beneath us and the sky above—these are all ingredients of mindfulness that are inherent in spending time with our horses. Thus we can see that our horses are wonderful meditation teachers. They are still in communion with the earth in a way that we humans have lost in our modern, technological world. Sharing time with horses can help us to find that connection again.

## *Teachers of nature*

As a Reiki practitioner, I've connected with lots of horses over the years, from high-level show horses to sanctuary and rescue horses. Horses have taught me so much about energy—about what it is, how it works, and why it's important to our healing. To me, horse energy is the perfect balance of earth and sky energies. Horses are so grounded and powerful—close to and rooted firmly to the earth. At the same time, the spirit of our horses is wild and free; they are sensitive to the more subtle, spiritual aspects of existence that might be difficult for us to connect to. In this way horses are expansive, like the sky. And so horses are our teachers of nature. Nature is a beautiful manifestation of healing and a balance of the earth and the sky—of things that we can see with our eyes, and things that we understand do exist but cannot see. Being with our horses brings us closer to this harmony of nature and our connections to the earth and to our subtle spirit, and so they are very healing for us.

## *Teachers of energy*

Being outside with our horses helps us become aware of the beauty of nature around us, which in turn helps us go to that quiet place inside us where healing energy flows so easily. Our true self, our inner essence, is composed of energy—that subtle force that lies at the center of all things. It's so hard for us humans to sense, yet our horses are powerfully in tune with this energy already—this is one of the reasons they are so responsive to sharing Reiki meditations. Connecting with our horses can help us become more aware of these more subtle aspects of existence. It takes a lot of practice, but with the help of our horse teachers, we can also learn to speak the language of energy. In reality, the language of energy is really just the language of the heart. When our hearts connect, this is the place where true healing can begin.

## *Teachers of "being in the flow"*

"Being in the flow" is a way of *being* in the world, no matter what we are *doing*—healing, riding, talking, walking, etc. —and the techniques of Reiki can help us to create this possibility of harmony in all that we do. If you spend time with horses, you are already practicing being in the flow, whether you realize it or not. That's because horses already live in the flow, and they help us to live there too, at least when we are with them.

For example, let's take a look at the similarities between sharing Reiki with a horse and riding in harmony with a horse. Sharing Reiki is about connection and Oneness. Interestingly enough, to be a good rider is also about becoming one with the horse—in essence, finding that energetic connection between two beings. As a rider, I try to use the same principles to excel that I use in my Reiki practice. I recently taught Reiki to my trainer, Susan, and we were talking about working with the energy and how it might be similar to what she already does in dressage. She started talking about the "quiet space" she goes to when she rides where all else falls away, and connection becomes effortless—the communication between horse and rider, the flow, just *being* together, and so on. As she spoke about it, I thought to myself: *This is exactly what I'm doing when I share Reiki with horses. I'm finding a quiet space inside myself, and in this space there is a connection with the horse where the healing can happen.*

The next time I rode, I thought about the similarities between Reiki and riding. When I first started sharing Reiki with horses I focused on Reiki's mechanics: where my hands were, if my hands were touching the horse or not, etc. I often felt pushback or resistance from a horse because I was trying so hard to "do" Reiki. In time and with practice, I was able to let go and just relax into the feeling of *being* Reiki, and letting the energy carry us both wherever it chose to. Similarly, while riding, as beginners we must first focus on the little details—our balance, the positions of our arms, legs, hands, shoulders, and so on. As we practice more, we can let go and clear our minds. When we manage to do this while we ride, everything falls into place, and it becomes almost effortless to ride correctly—our horses become happy and responsive as they feel us becoming more in tune with them. This is the same kind of appreciation I receive from horses when I'm sharing Reiki with them. They give me such a beautiful kind of attention and kindness, as if they are saying, "Wow, I've been waiting for a person to really listen and connect to me on a deeper level."

Riding in perfect harmony is one way to experience how we are all connected to each other. Reiki is just another way to access this connection. Practicing Reiki techniques can help us develop our connection to that quiet space inside of us where all these wonderful possibilities exist; where we learn to deepen our bonds with the horses we love.

## <u>Case Study:</u> *Horse Healing*
## by Emma Duvefelt

Early spring mornings can be quite cold in northern Maine. On one of those mornings, when I went out to the barn to feed the goats and horse their breakfasts, I found the smallest goat, Alouette, standing quietly, head and tail down, too cold to move. The other two goats were standing nearby. P, our horse, was watching from her stall.

I turned up the overhead barn heater, put some fresh hay in front of Alouette, and ran back to the house to get some warm water and a heavier coat for myself. When I returned, in great haste, Alouette had nestled down under the heater and the other two goats were lying near her, making small chanting sounds. P was eating her hay quietly, keeping an eye on her goats.

I poured some warm water for the goats. Alouette had stopped shivering. Her twin sister was lying near her, their heads almost touching. A third goat was lying not far away. I sat myself down and prepared to share some Reiki. I focused on my breathing, bringing my breath deep into my hara. Occasionally a worried thought would pass through my mind, but I continued to breathe slowly and deeply—or so I thought.

The goats stopped their chanting, and P began to toss her hay around, obviously irritated, moving restlessly. Something was wrong. I stopped and listened with all of my senses. I realized I had barged in to a healing space that the goats and P had created on their own. I was surrounded by the vast, gentle space they had already created for Alouette. As I got up to leave, the goats resumed their chanting and P again began to quietly eat her hay. In my humanness I had thought that I needed to be the one to save the day. Not so. Not so at all.

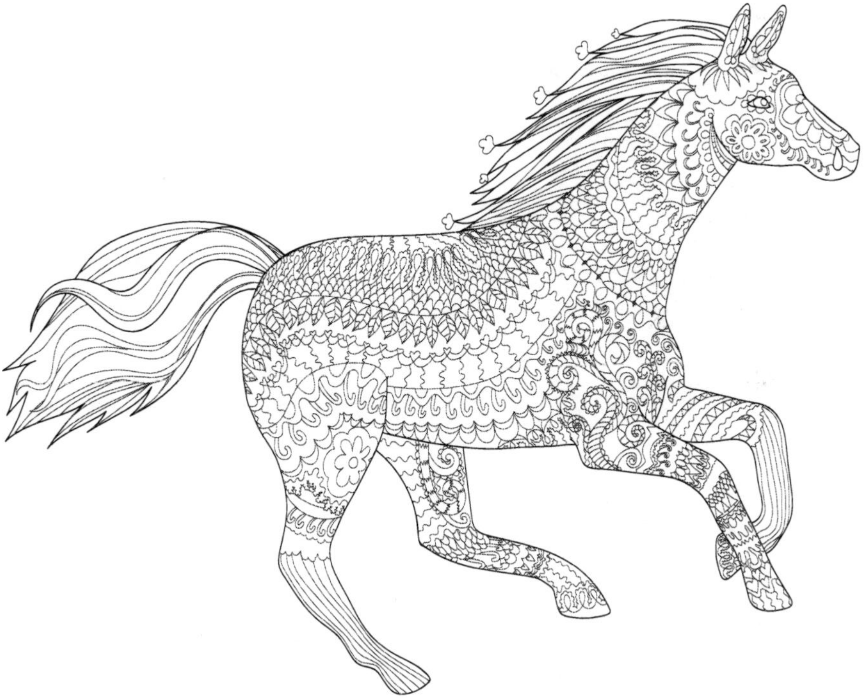

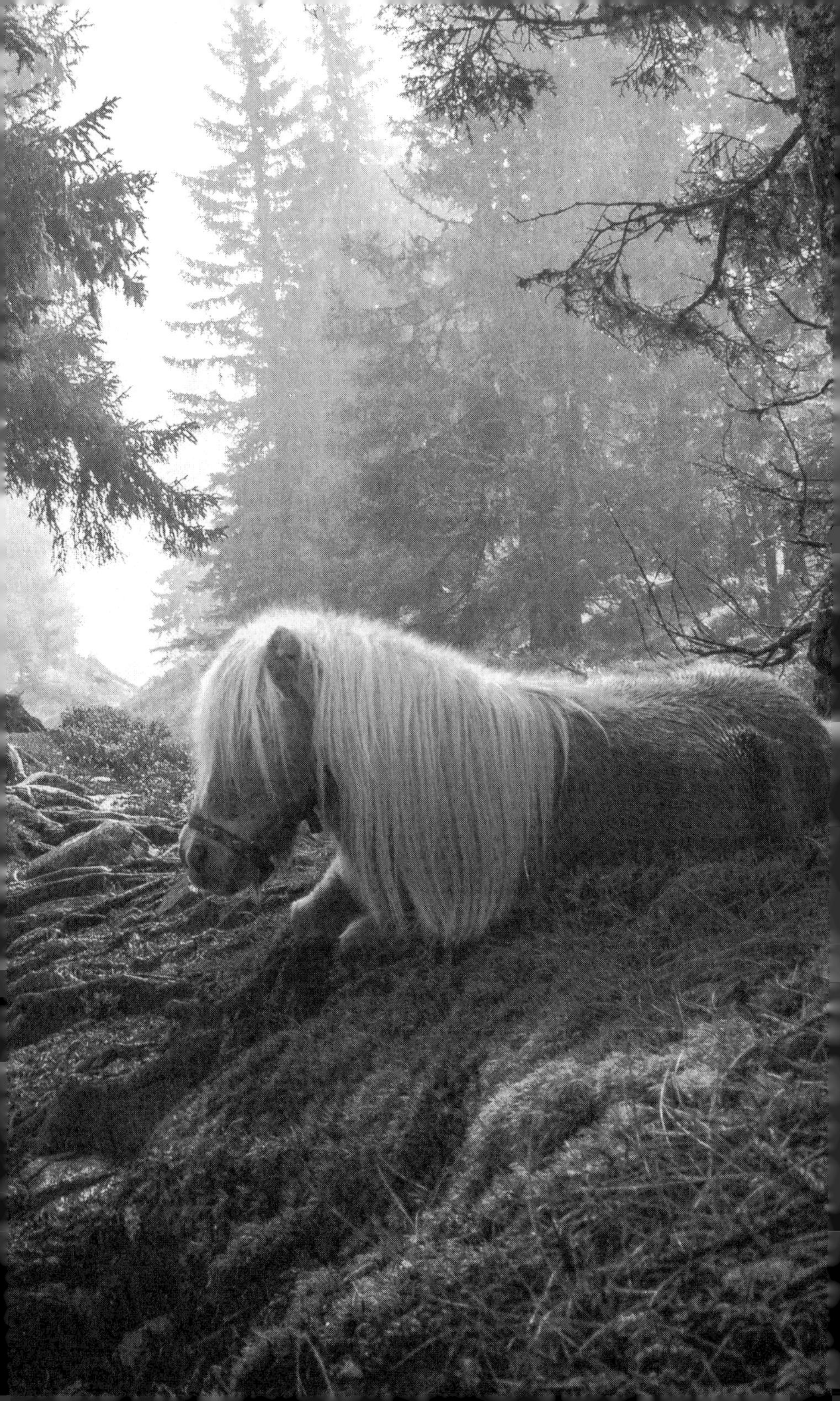

## Being Peace with Your Horse Meditation

Open yourself to the energy of peace and calm that surrounds you. Stand outside your horse's paddock or pasture in a comfortable position, spine straight, shoulders and arms relaxed. Your eyes should remain open and in soft focus. Place your hands over your lower belly. Relax your entire body as you breathe deeply a few times. Imagine there are roots growing down from the base of your spine, deep and wide into the earth. Imagine that the powerful, grounding energy of the earth can flow up these roots into your lower belly, giving you stability and peace. Take ten breaths, and on each inhale, feel peaceful earth energy coming up into your lower belly. On each exhale, release any emotions, fears, or worries you may have out through your roots, easily dissolving them into the peacefulness that is earth energy. With each successive breath, feel more and more stillness and stability within you. Once you have completed the ten breaths, allow yourself to relax in the space of earth energy and stability that you have created with your breath.

Once you feel fully calm and connected to the earth, simply invite your horse into the peaceful space you have created with your breath. Imagine that within this space, all is perfect and balanced, and that your horse can join you there. Feel harmony enveloping both you and your horse. Let go of your expectations, along with any worries about what needs to be healed, and continue to breathe the calm and strength of earth energy into your belly as you share this space with your horse.

Notice if your horse comes closer or stays farther away. Place your hands gently on your horse if he approaches, or keep them on your belly if he chooses to remain at a distance. Signs of relaxation and stress relief in your horse will indicate that he is sharing your peaceful healing space with you.

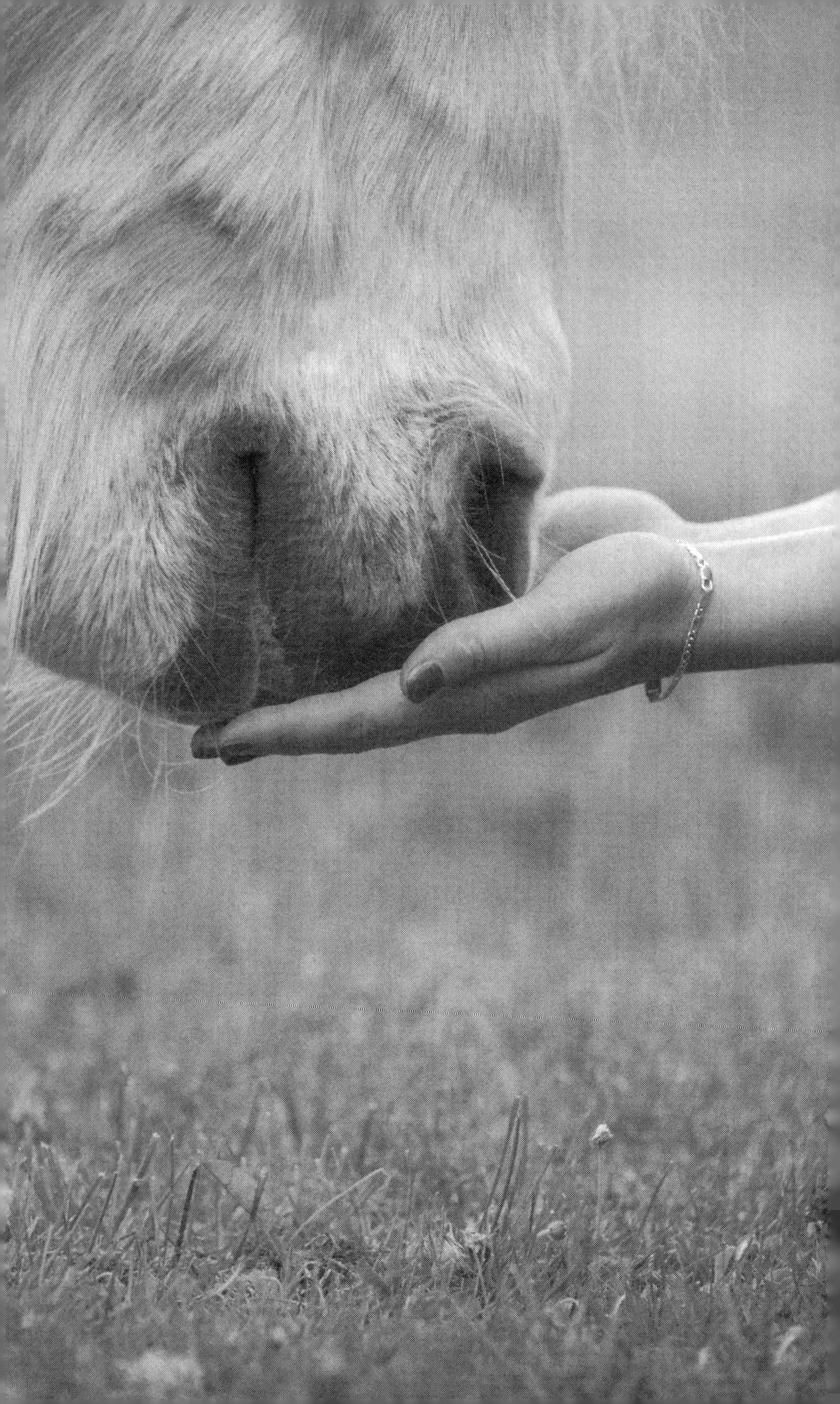

## CHAPTER 6
# State of Mind

*Keep your heart clear*
*And transparent,*
*And you will*
*Never be bound.*
*A single disturbed thought*
*Creates ten thousand distractions.*

—Ryokan

THIS QUOTE DESCRIBES the essential connection between our mind and the clarity and power of the heart. The state of your thoughts and emotions must be considered if you want to create a powerful heart connection when sharing Reiki with animals. Relaxation, patience, and positivity: these three qualities are key in developing a state of *being* where the healing power of your heart can flourish. By maintaining an open mind and heart, we can create conditions where horses are receptive to sharing Reiki.

Horses are very sensitive to our mental and emotional states. If our thoughts or emotions are disturbed, a horse will know it;

we cannot possibly hide it from them. If we are tense, rushing, worried, or angry, this may be a reason for some horses to say "no thanks" to connecting with us. For example, rescued horses who have been through a lot and don't know us can be easily put off by our disturbed state of mind. As much as possible, if we can stabilize our inner being, finding a quiet, grounded, and peaceful place within ourselves, we will create ideal conditions for horses to say yes to connecting heart to heart for healing.

How do we do this? Not by frantically grasping at straws while in the moment of emotion, upset, or chaos, but rather, through dedication to our own daily personal meditation practice. By meditating daily, we practice going deeper into our own essence and healing our own issues so that our energy flows clearer and brighter while also growing our roots and strengthening our energetic center so that it remains stable no matter what situation we may find ourselves in. In this way, when we do find ourselves surrounded by upset, emotion, or chaos, our inner calm and center can come to the surface much more easily, because we have created a stable relationship with them through our practice.

### *Learning to focus inward: Developing relaxation*

> *"Turn around the light to shine within, then just return… Let go of hundreds of years and relax completely. Open your hands and walk, innocent."*
>
> —Shitou/Sekito

I love this quote because as human beings, we often make everything so complicated. Yet the best way to create a strong connection with our horses is simply to let go and *be*. As previously stated, sharing Reiki with our horses is not an outward activity of *doing*, rather, it is an inward mental state of *being*, an intention to peel back our own layers to find our true nature, the nature that is our Oneness with all beings. In accessing this reality of connectedness, we also access infinite healing potential and possibility. Meditation gives us the path that leads into this healing potential, showing us how to relax into the softness and gentleness of Reiki, the healing energetic space that exists all around us, rather than trying so hard to *do* and *fix*, and push energy this way and that way.

Recently my trainer's horse Luke had to go to a nearby veterinary hospital for surgery to remove bladder stones. When I arrived at the barn, everyone there was waiting for the trailer to arrive, a bit stressed and worried. Susan asked me to share Reiki with Luke, and I knew I had to somehow let go of my own distracted mind and upset emotions in order to be able to support him.

I started by going into the tack room and spending several minutes practicing Reiki *hara* breathing. I could feel myself becoming more grounded and calm with each breath. When I felt ready, I quietly walked to Luke's stall, imagining I could bring this peaceful space with me. I stepped into his stall and saw that he was in the attached outdoor paddock. Rather than approaching him directly, I stayed inside, near the door, and placed my hands over my lower belly and closed my eyes. Almost immediately, I heard Luke's footsteps as he walked into the indoor stall and approached me, placing his nose against my hands. We stood like this for several minutes, very peaceful and connected. He sighed and his breath became very calm.

After several minutes, my mind began to wander. I started to think again of the trip to the veterinary hospital, worrying about Luke's surgery and the possible outcomes, etc. No sooner did these thoughts pass through my mind than Luke's head popped up and he quickly turned around and marched outside to his paddock. I realized what I had done, and silently went back to my hara breathing, focusing my energy on the energy center in my lower belly, to help recenter and rebalance. After just a few minutes I felt myself becoming more stable again, and almost immediately, Luke reentered the stall and placed his nose against my chest. I put my hands on his head and we stood there together in perfect relaxation and peacefulness.

After several more minutes, my mind wandered again. I began to think about my hand placement, wondering if I should put my hands near Luke's bladder instead of on his head. This reminded of his problem, and I began to feel worried. Once again, at the same instant I became mentally distracted and emotionally unbalanced, Luke's head popped up and he turned quickly and marched out of the stall, away from me.

This scenario repeated itself a handful of times in our forty-five-minute session. Each time, Luke was completely aware of my thoughts emotions. He only wanted to connect with me when I was able to let go, focus inward, and relax. This was such an amazing lesson for me—I will always be grateful to Luke! I am happy to say that the surgery successfully removed his bladder stones, and he is happy and healthy again.

## *Giving a horse choice: Developing patience*

The novelist Paulo Coelho once said, "Why is patience so important? Because it makes us pay attention." Patience is especially important when we are with a horse during a Reiki session. If we are pushing our ideas about how we think the horse should act or ways the horse needs to heal, how soon, and so on, we create lots of judgment and expectations, which the horses will pick up on. It can feel to the horse that we are not listening, not giving them ownership of their own healing process. This can make them very uncomfortable, and perhaps even unwilling to connect with us.

When we forget patience, we are coming from a very human place of, "Okay, here I am ready to heal you; let's get this done!" and then our focus shifts to our ego rather than the horse's well-being. The deepest heart to heart healing with horses happens when we give them choice, sharing Reiki with them by just being present, waiting and allowing, surrendering and observing, as a supportive witness, rather than a doer. When we learn to trust the process, we will also receive a special gift: a deepening of our own intuitive knowing. In learning to quietly and patiently observe healing as it naturally unfolds, we can become acquainted with a deeper layer of the horse's being that we otherwise might have missed.

Recently, while I was teaching an equine Reiki class, one of the students asked if I could demonstrate some typical hand positions that might be used during a session. So I took the students out into a field where several horses stood. As they gathered in front of me, I began by saying, "Well, it's important that we find a willing participant who won't mind being the demonstration horse for all of you today. We wouldn't want to force this on anyone; remember that we only do hands-on Reiki when the animal initiates it." As I was speaking, one of the horses walked right up and stood next to me, waiting for me to begin the demonstration! The students laughed, and I said, "Well, clearly we have a volunteer." I proceeded to show a variety of hand positions that a horse might ask for, and as soon as I had finished, the horse walked away.

What if the horses that day had said no thanks to the demonstration? I would have been patient and accepting of their disinterest. I could have discussed the topic with the students in a descriptive fashion and still gotten the point across, even without a horse model. It's much more important to me to honor the choices of animals in each and every situation than to impose my own will on them simply so I can demonstrate a hand position.

It always amazes me how much horses appreciate when we approach them with choice, not putting our own designs on them. Often they will take their time, testing us to see whether we are really offering them a choice, and then choose to come forward in their own time *only* because we have truly left it up to them. When we choose *for* them, when we rush them by approaching them with our human schedule, they may say no thanks! It's hard for humans to learn patience, to let go of our own timeline and our proclivity for doing—but the rewards are so big when we do!

I remember once in a Level 1 Reiki class I taught at Bright-Haven, I took the students out into one of the horse pastures to practice. I gave them a Reiki meditation to focus on and reminded them to just hold the space, no matter what happened. We formed a very large circle in the pasture, near the herd of horses. As soon as we began our meditation, the horses quickly walked away—every single one! They marched all the way to the barn, out of our sight.

I could see the students looking at me for direction, and I could tell some of them were already ending their meditation. I simply smiled and put my hands on my lower belly and continued with my *hara* breathing. The students looked at one another, shrugged their shoulders, and began their *hara* breath again. Some of them even closed their eyes, given that there were no horses to look at anymore. The pasture became incredibly peaceful as the students slowly let go of their expectations and relaxed.

Within about five minutes, something amazing happened: The herd came back to us! One by one the horses walked slowly across the pasture all the way back to our circle and greeted each student by touching their muzzles to hand or body, then moving to the next student. Once all of the students had been greeted by each horse, the horses relaxed and began grazing again, some inside our circle, some outside but nearby. I could see the students smiling in amazement. Patience really does pay off!

## *Seeing deeper than the surface: Developing positivity*

I believe that all of us consist of a beautiful inner essence of light. This light remains perfect and timeless, stretching beyond this lifetime even as it exists for a short time in this physical body. When we are with horses who may benefit from our Reiki support, it is helpful to let go of our eyes and look deeper, seeing them with our hearts, as the beautiful bright lights that are their inner essences. This is who they really are—not their mortal shells, not their physical, emotional struggles. It's so easy to forget this, to instead begin to identify them as their problems we see on the surface. Remember that underneath the surface, the bright inner light that is the essence of their being is already perfect and balanced. If we can see this perfect light within our horses, and hold that vision in our minds and hearts as we offer to share Reiki with them, this can help give them the support they need to remember their inner strength and heal themselves.

Remembering to see animals, people, and situations with our hearts rather than our eyes will help us to create a positive state of mind that will be felt by every being who is sharing the Reiki session, including the animal's people. This positivity is key not only to earning an animal's trust but also to supporting the inner strength and courage of the animal's people as they walk with their animal through the healing journey.

One special horse at BrightHaven named Nicki taught many students about positivity. Nicki was what I like to call a "Reiki sponge." She loved Reiki so much that she would fall asleep almost immediately whenever any of us would go into the pasture to share Reiki. Nicki had severe arthritis and had difficulty moving around. The first response many students had when they saw her was, "Oh, the poor thing!" However, after meditating with her, you couldn't help but smile—she was such a sweet spirit. Although Nicki's body continued to weaken and eventually gave out, her heart was so gentle and open that everyone who spent time with her could feel her peacefulness and love. Even in her passing, she brought beautiful gifts of peace and freedom to those around her.

Richard Pope, co-founder of BrightHaven, remembers his last moments with Nicki:

"I settled down, comfortable in my vigil, with arms wrapped lightly around Nicki's neck and my head resting gently thereon. We were at peace there together in the still–early morning cold air. It was then that I suddenly became aware of a single gray dove who had landed just a few feet away from Nicki's great head and seemed to be gazing right at us both. Time passed, and eventually the dove turned and gently flew westward toward the horizon whilst we watched with never a movement, until she could be seen no more.

Suddenly, Nicki leaned her great head back and around to stare deeply into my eyes for several moments. She then turned her head again in the direction of the dove, at which time her legs began to gently run. She looked back intently at my face one more time, turned again, and left—forever."

When we look deeper than the surface of things, it becomes much easier to get in touch with our heart, to know that our heart's journey continues beyond the lifetime that we can see with our eyes. How wonderful to be able to see death as a journey into spirit, rather than an ending—for when we look deeper than the surface we can see that we are never truly separated from each other when we are connecting through our hearts.

### *The key: practice, practice, practice!*

*There is a bright pearl within me,*
*Buried for a long time under dust.*

*Today, the dust is gone and the light radiates,*
*Shining through all the mountains and rivers.*

—Master Yueh of Ch'a-ling

Doing your daily meditation practice is like dusting your bright pearl, uncovering your inner light. Success in connecting with horses is fundamentally tied to your own discipline in working on your own self-healing. Keep visiting this peaceful inner Reiki space over and over again. Invite your horse to be your daily meditation partner—practice standing in the pasture or in their paddock or stall and letting go of everything; just be in the moment, be with your breath, and be with your horse. Let go, let go, and let go, over and over, every day. You will be building your meditation muscles and developing a stable mental and emotional state of peaceful relaxation, patience, and positivity that your horses will gravitate towards. In time, this inner peace will radiate outward without effort—it will simply become who you are, and when a difficult situation arises, you will more easily be able to stay strong and grounded through it.

## **Case Study: *Reiki and Grief***
## **by Carol A. Hulse**

When Kathleen asked who wanted to work with the horses for our inaugural animal Reiki session at the May 2010 Reiki I workshop at BrightHaven Animal Sanctuary, I surprised myself by eagerly raising my hand. Don't get me wrong—I think horses are wonderful beings. However, I sometimes feel intimidated by their sheer size.

Tears welled in my eyes as we approached three horses contentedly grazing in a paddock. My grief over the death of my beloved husband, Martin, four years before had been on the surface for me throughout the weekend. My emotion also sprang from the sacredness I felt surrounding my first animal Reiki experience at magical BrightHaven.

As I shared Reiki with Bellestar, a Shetland pony, tears started to flow down my cheeks. When I shared my experience with Kathleen, who was standing nearby, she told me that Nicki, a special horse and prominent barnyard personality at BrightHaven, had recently died. After centering myself with hara breathing, I quickly realized I was also experiencing grief other than my own. I felt strong and confident in the knowledge that I could feel the emotions of others and not be overwhelmed by those feelings. Bellestar taught me that I could be fully present and helpful to others in their healing process.

Perhaps Bellestar was able to release some of her grief over Nicki's death as we were enveloped by healing Reiki energy. I know I relinquished some of my own sorrow in that beautiful space.

## Case Study: *Paiute Horses*
## by Cathy O'Brien

I was at a Reiki class at a horse sanctuary called Pregnant Mare Rescue. They had recently taken in four wild foals who were rescued from a slaughter truck after a roundup. They were still scared and mistrustful of people. Three of us were standing in a large pasture sharing Reiki. We were at one end of the pasture, while the foals were standing in a far corner, quietly eating, watching us warily and keeping their distance.

While practicing Reiki, I felt a very strong hot flash coming on, the kind that zaps your all energy. I felt dizzy, and needed to sit down. I walked over to the very far end of the pasture and found a tree stump where I could sit.

Suddenly, one of the foals looked at me, and walked all the way over to where I was sitting. He put his face right up to mine, and I very clearly felt him asking me if I was OK. I thanked him for his concern and told him I was fine, that I just needed to sit for a moment. He let me give him a little stroke on his neck, and then he walked back over to his friends and continued eating.

I was awestruck. The gentleness, love, and compassion I felt from this young horse —after all he had been through at the hands of people—brought tears to my eyes. I was overcome with love and gratitude. I realized at that moment that when we share Reiki with an animal, it is an energy exchange, not something we are doing *to* them. It is a connection that goes both ways. And when an animal allows us in like that, it is a gift to be cherished.

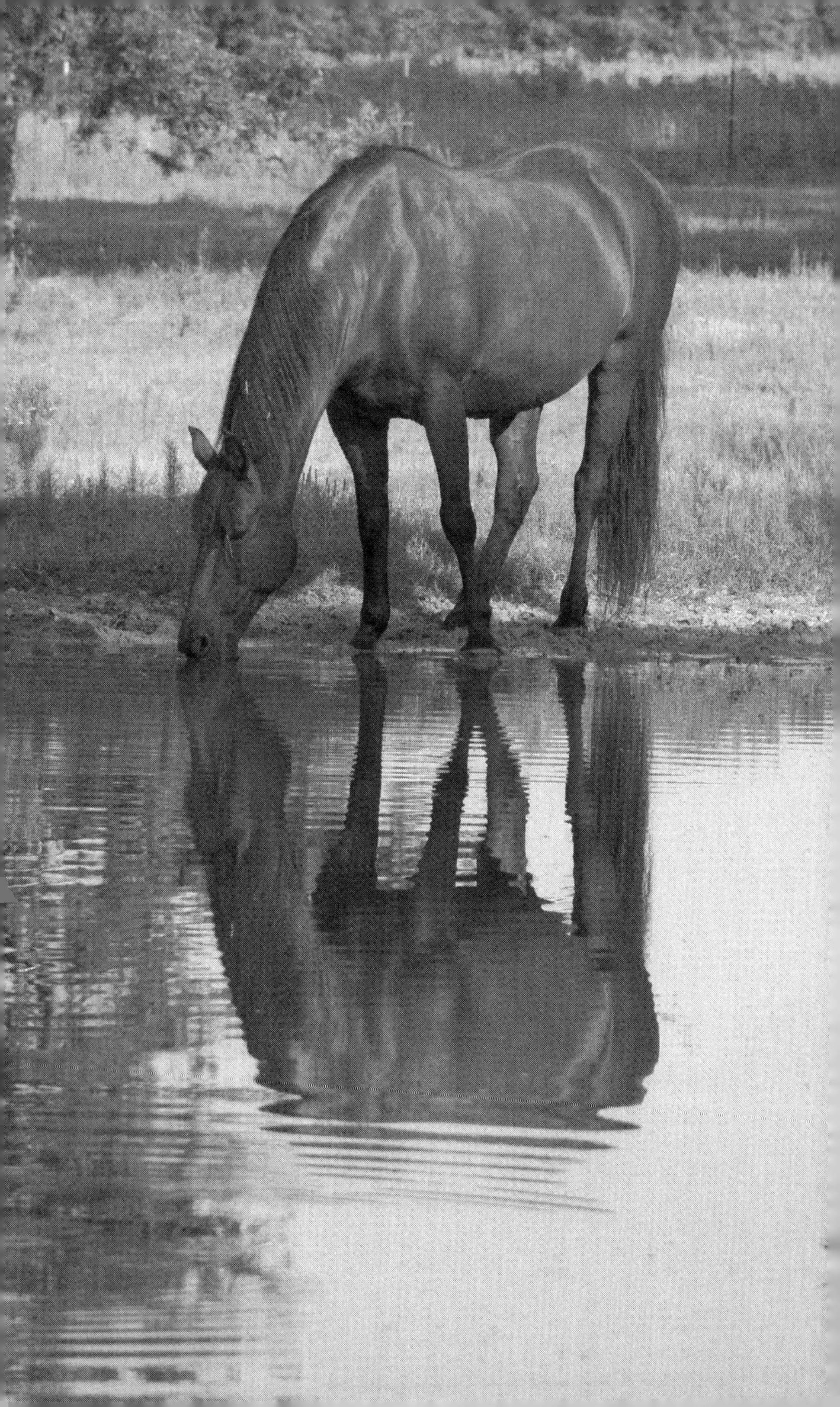

# The Healing Pond Meditation
## (Developing a Gentle and Open State of Mind)

Symbolically, water represents strength through change, strength through remaining formless. The water on the surface of a pond may be still and peaceful, clear and pure, yet it is also very deep, and under the surface there can be much movement from the creatures who call the pond home. In the same way, Reiki with your horse can appear quiet on the surface—as if you are doing nothing at all but standing with your horse—and yet, when we look deeper, amazing healing may be happening just beneath the surface.

When we look at a pond, we can see the sky reflected in its surface—the pond is at once grounded in physical nature and reality, while at the same time reflecting heaven and sky above, the essence of open, limitless space and possibility. Similarly, when we are with a horse in the Reiki space we can connect in this physical moment, while also connecting to the spiritual dimension in which limitless healing possibility exists.

In one way, a pond remains the same over time—we can always count on it being there as seasons and years pass—but in another way, every time we look at it, it reflects something different: blue or gray skies, storm clouds, sun, or rainbows. The pond will always be a mirror of this present moment in time. Similarly, we can learn to be present and open to whatever this very moment with our horse may look like, without judgment, worry, or clinging, with love and compassion and openness.

As you stand with your horse, imagine you can pour all your light and love—your compassionate intention—into a pond. Then, simply invite your horse to come and drink from this healing pond, as they wish and as they are comfortable. Remember to relax, be patient, and remain positive. Just be in the moment with your horse. It is in this quiet, open state of mind that all healing possibility exists.

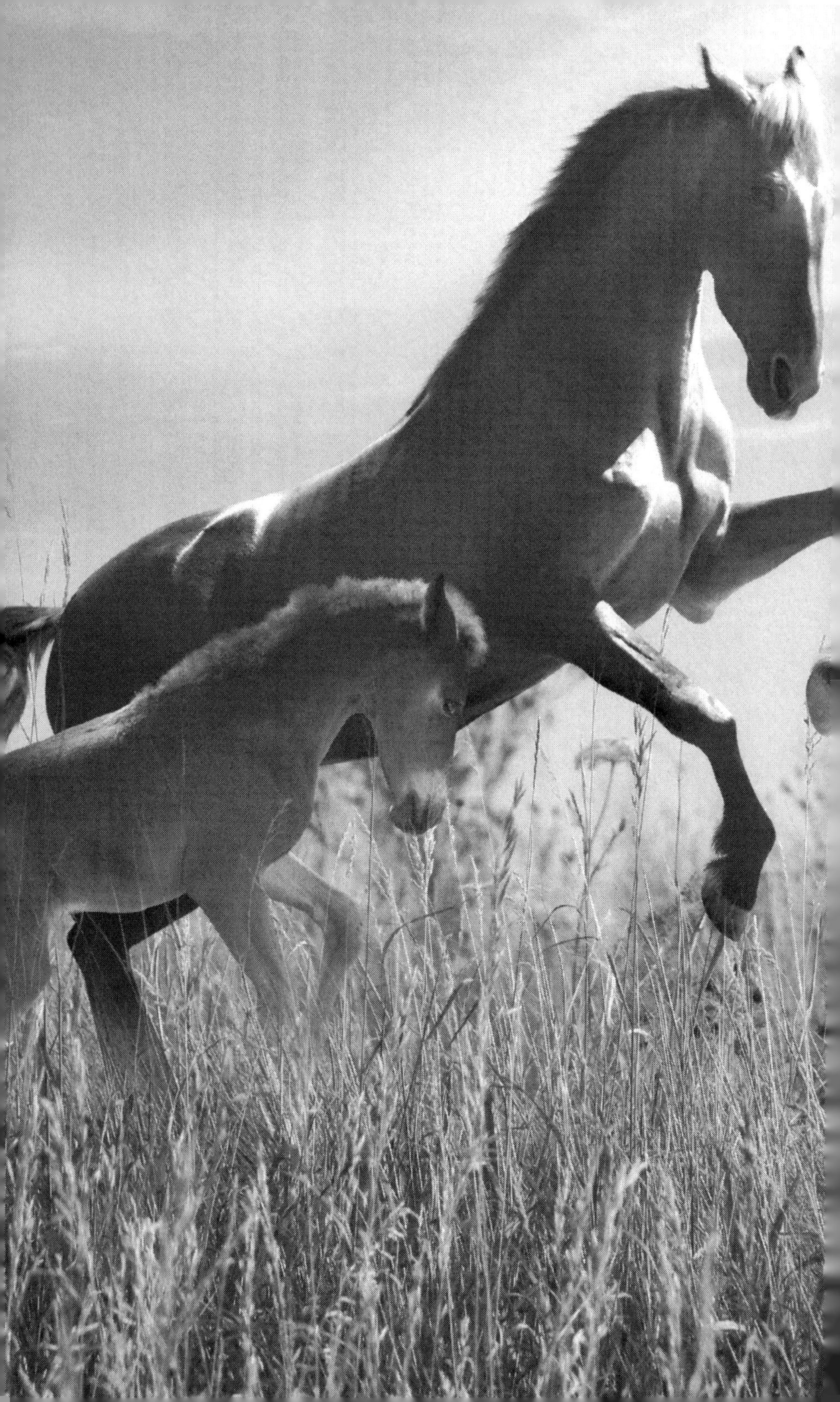

## CHAPTER 7

# Three Ways to Nurture Your Horse's Spirit, And Your Own

*"In difficulty, there is opportunity."*

—Ray Hunt

REIKI PRACTICE GIVES us the tools to transform difficult moments into healing opportunities. Just as my own state of mind and emotions affect my health and wellbeing, so does my horse's affect his. If his thoughts and emotions are out of balance, it will be very difficult for him to heal himself. Reiki meditation provides a wonderful opportunity for us to help our horse shift out of suffering into a positive inner state—in other words, Reiki boosts your horse's spirit so that healing can manifest. Below are three ways you can help nurture your companion horse's spirit, and thus strengthen his healing potential.

**Way 1:** Transform your shadow horse into a radiant horse.

If we want to help our horses find true healing, we need to encourage their spirits, their positive inner states. To do this, we must first cultivate our own positive perception of our horses, so that we may see their spirits more clearly. Let's use the image of a "spirit horse" to help us visualize how the positive and negative aspects of our inner thoughts and emotions affect healing potential and possibility. This horse consists of two parts: a radiant horse and a shadow horse, which are intimately connected to each other. Our radiant horse represents all the best qualities of the heart: those positive aspects of ourselves that help us to get through even the most difficult of times. Our shadow horse represents the unconscious worries and fears that shape our negative reactions when we ourselves or those we love are faced with suffering of any kind.

Our shadow horse is not grounded and is very fearful. The slightest breeze will spook him. This is because we forget to call upon the ancient wisdom of earth to help us remember that we are all connected, and that in this connection there is great strength. We forget that at our deepest level, in our energetic essence, we have limitless healing potential. We forget that our beautiful inner light is always perfect and bright and eternal, no matter what struggles our mortal shell may be facing. This is very important to remember, and yet when we ourselves, or those we love, are hurting, it is very easy to forget.

Our shadow horse has no sunlight, no expansive compassionate sky above him. Our ego is a dark cloud above this horse. Our ego wants control over the healing process, wants to fix every problem, and wants to say, "If I do this and that, nothing bad will ever happen to me or anyone I love." Our ego manifests like heavy saddlebags, weighing down our shadow horse, and our fears cause these saddlebags to multiply. Expectation weighs down our shadow horse. Control is another weight, blame is yet another. When we or those we care about are in pain, we create all kinds of expectations, wanting to control the situation and its outcome, or we try to find something to blame for why it is happening. The piling on of worry, disappointment, frustration, anxiety, denial, depression, anger, sadness, defeat, and so on causes our shadow horse to become paralyzed to do anything to assist in a difficult situation. Perhaps we will run in the opposite direction, or if we stay, we might find it impossible to find the positive amidst a difficult situation.

For many of us, this shadow horse is the only way we know how to face our own hardships or the distress of those we love. This is because unconsciously we are nurturing our shadow horse by giving our ego permission to practice fear, worry, and control on a daily basis in our lives, hoping that somehow this shadow will sustain us in difficult times.

The many spiritual practices of Reiki can help us to heal our inner shadow horse, and to help it transform into a strong and powerful radiant horse of courage, wisdom, and compassion. Manifesting this inner positive transformation of heart and mind means we will be able to support the companion horses in our lives, no matter what health issues they may face. This compassionate support is the strongest kind of healing we can offer to them!

How do we transform our shadow horse into a radiant horse? The Reiki precepts, healing sessions, Reiki meditations, and Reiju can all help shift our state of mind and heart. Practicing Reiki daily can help us to develop an unshakeable core and a root system of wisdom from the earth, while also helping us to reach out into the sky beyond the clouds so that compassion can shine upon us. Practicing Reiki creates the mix of wisdom and compassion in our spirit and promotes a shining peacefulness that can radiate out into the world around us for the benefit of others.

The deepest power of practicing Reiki lies in its ability to strengthen our center of spiritual wellness. When we regularly practice positive qualities such as peace, wisdom, grounding, compassion and gratitude, we develop and boost our spirits. As our spirits move towards balance, our minds and bodies will also feel the ripple effects, and we will see shifts towards healing on all levels. When we feed and water our radiant horse with Reiki practice, it will not only sustain and carry us forward, but also help us to assist others. Our companion horses can always sense our emotional and spiritual balance (or lack of balance). Nurture your inner radiant horse first, in order to aid your companion horse's spirit!

To help you transform your shadow horse, invite horse wisdom into your meditation. Imagine all the wisdom of horses past and present as a beautiful light that can fill your shadow horse so that it shines like the sun. This light represents all the strength and courage horses have shown through the ages. Within this light, the shadow dissipates and loses all its power.

Visualize this radiant horse with you as you sit with your companion horse who is ill, or if you are ill yourself, see this radiant horse standing with you. Imagine your horse can step into the light if he wishes, for perfect healing. Envisioning this radiant horse can help you to remember you are not alone and can awaken your inner power and strength, as well as your ancient connection to horse wisdom inside yourself. You can navigate your own health challenges and those of your horses with grace, calm, and courage!

### 2. Transform your perspective on illness.

Just as we can transform our shadow horse into a radiant horse, we can also transform the way we view illness itself. This quote by Sogyal Rinpoche expresses the philosophy behind this transformation beautifully:

*"The times when you are suffering can be those when you*

*are open, and where you are extremely vulnerable can be where your greatest strength really lies. Say to yourself: 'I am not going to run away from this suffering. I want to use it in the best and richest way I can, so that I can become more compassionate and more helpful to others.' Suffering, after all, can teach us about compassion. If you suffer, you will know how it is when others suffer. And if you are in a position to help others, it is through your suffering that you will find the understanding and compassion to do so."*

To transform your perspective on illness, you must practice seeing your own illness as a source of strength, as a gift that you can use to help others. When you are suffering, remember you are not the only one suffering with illness—there are many others. In fact, many others are much worse off than you are. Remembering this can begin to shift your focus from your own suffering to compassion for the suffering of others. Compassion is different from pity, where we might just feel sorry for the horse and see ourselves separate from him. With compassion, we let go of judgment, open the heart and lean into the heart to heart connection. There is an incredible amount of peace and healing to be found through the unity that compassion connection brings, heart to heart!

In addition to recognizing the spiritual gifts that illness can bring, it is also good to practice seeing the illness of your companion horse as only the outer layer of his/her being. Allow yourself to look deeper and realize that inside, your horse companion is beautiful, bright, and perfect already. In other words, we are not defined by our illnesses. I like to call this way of looking at illness as "seeing with our Reiki eyes," but what I really mean is that when we see illness in this way we learn to see with our hearts. Our horses are our teachers in this, because they already know how to see with their Reiki eyes: just think of how your horse sees you, without judgment and without expectation. Even when we are weak or sick, our horse companions still see through to our hearts.

### 3. Transform difficult moments into compassionate moments.

> *"The sun of real happiness shines in your life when you start to cherish others."*
>
> —Lama Zopa Rinpoche

Compassion is why we are here on this planet. Compassion heals from the inside out, and therefore it is the key to healing all illness. I like to say, "Peaceful heart, peaceful mind, peaceful horses." When we ourselves are in a peaceful state, our peacefulness ripples out to touch all those around us. This ripple effect is the healing power of compassion.

In modern society, healing illness is most often seen as being about healing the outer surface of things, our physical bodies. We mostly deal with illness by suppressing symptoms, rather than healing the origin of the problem. Reiki teaches us that the deepest form of healing is not about our bodies at all. True and lasting healing is about our hearts and minds; however, all healing is connected. So if you want to heal illness in the body—whether for yourself or for the horses you love in your life—the process has to start with healing the heart and mind, and developing peacefulness. Reiki practice, in all its aspects, nurtures peacefulness and the healing of heart and mind, and therefore is a very useful method to attain the deep healing of compassion, which can also heal illness.

Imagine you can look inside yourself, into your spiritual center, and see your shadow horse and your radiant horse there. If you also now visualize the power of Reiki in your life, how does it affect these inner horses? For me, Reiki is the sun shining so brightly in the sky over these horses that it can illuminate all the shadows, dissipating all the fear, the expectations, ego, anger, worry, hope and other saddlebag feelings that weigh them down. Reiki shines a light on these emotional experiences so that we can see them for what they are, and slowly let them go. Then we can transform ourselves, lighten ourselves, bit by bit. With Reiki practice, our shadow horse loses its heavy weight and can become radiant. Expectation transforms into surrender, ego into compassion, hope into joy, denial into acceptance, depression into peace, anger into tranquility, worry into confidence, and so on. Before we know it, through our daily practice, our shadow horse has become the strongest, most courageous radiant horse!

This change will happen naturally and easily when we learn to shine. It is only because we don't see our own inner spirits clearly that we approach life from a place of fear. It is only due to the dark clouds of ego that we can't remember peace. And yet, underneath it all, even when we feel at our weakest, our true inner self is always ready to burst forth with healing, with the most brilliant and radiant light of wisdom and compassion. Lucky for us, when we are sick or suffering, our horses can still see our inner hearts.

*"Perhaps the greatest gift an animal has to offer is a permanent reminder of who we really are."*

—Nick Trout

Besides being reminded by our horses, the practices of Reiki can help us to remember this inner light. And when we learn to shine, we can be a mirror for our horses to remember their inner lights as well. We aren't the only ones who can serve as mirrors; horses often do this effortlessly for us.

Once, several years ago, I taught a Reiki class at Bright-

Haven in which one of the students had very low self-confidence. Because she had been through a lot of tragedy in her life, she didn't believe that she would have anything to offer to the horses, although she wanted very much to help them. I took the students out to the pasture where the horses were eating, and invited them each to go stand near a horse and practice their meditation. Each student chose a horse to stand near, but when this particular student approached her horse, the horse walked quickly away, leaving her standing there alone. She was very discouraged and stopped the exercise, and went to go stand by the gate and wait for us to all leave.

The horse I was standing with was Mocha, an amazing, compassionate being. I looked at Mocha, looked at my student, and thought in my mind, "Can you help?" Immediately Mocha lifted her head from her hay to look at me intently. She then purposefully walked all the way across the pasture to the student standing at the fence and stood with her for several minutes. The student's smile returned and, her confidence regained, she continued with the meditation. As Mocha slowly walked back to her hay, I invited the student to join her, and sure enough, Mocha continued to share a beautiful connection with the student for the entire hour. It was really something to see! After the exercise, this student shared with the group that she had initially given up on the idea of sharing energy with the horses, but when Mocha sought her out, she began to feel the connection of Reiki, and felt very inspired now to try to share Reiki with other animals!

This is the gift that Mocha was able to give this student—simply to remind her of her inner light, her inner connection, her inner joy and peacefulness. When we choose to connect with horses and to share our lives with them, they can help us to develop our inner light, and our ability to heal. For those of us who have loved a horse, we know they help us to open our hearts more fully, they show us how to love unconditionally, how to be present and mindful and let go of judgment. Horses are great teachers of compassion.

> *"Each place is the right place—the place where I now am can be a sacred space."*
>
> —Ravi Ravindra

In order to transform a struggle in our own lives or in the lives of our companion horses, we must practice being at peace with what is, yet remember that all things are possible. If we are facing a difficulty ourselves, do we fall apart and give up, or do we use that experience to make ourselves stronger and help others? Gratitude for the spiritual experience we gain from our own suffering and healing process can help us find our compassion. If we are helping a very ill horse, are we able to create a peaceful space, without expectation and fear, to share with him/her? Whether a horse's body will heal or whether perhaps it is his/her time to pass, wouldn't it be a beautiful gift to support that process with peace and compassion? Allow Reiki and your love for your horses to help you to remember your gratitude and create a sacred, compassionate space in this present moment, whatever it looks like.

## Case Study: *Touching Hearts with a Pony*
## by Ann Noyce

> *"All I ever wanted was to reach out and touch another human being not just with my hands but with my heart."*
>
> —Tahereh Mafi, *Shatter Me*

A Shetland pony named Pete twice taught me the meaning of the precept, "Be compassionate to yourself and others." Being compassionate, as I've learned, is reaching out to others with our hearts and not just our actions.

I was asked to assist Pete in overcoming his fear of people. As I shared a Reiki space with Pete, I could see deeper than his outer fearful behavior. I wanted to see him with my heart, not just my eyes. Underneath, I saw a very sweet pony with a very big heart. In this Reiki connection, he could interact with me and connect in the energy in whatever way he felt comfortable. I focused on peace and harmony. After a few minutes, I could feel his fears begin to melt away as he opened his heart in trust to me. He eventually came forward to stand next to me. This was wonderful, but then, even more amazingly, he leaned his body against mine in total relaxation. Through Reiki, I was able to open my heart to Pete and gain his trust. Reiki was able to create a beautiful heart to heart connection between us.

A few months later, I saw Pete again. On this particular day, I was feeling a bit stressed and overwhelmed. When Pete saw me, he quickly came over to the fence, whinnying, calling me over to see him. As I rubbed his muzzle, I felt a warm heart energy surrounding me. I felt my demeanor shift; I felt the stress melt away. I felt calmer, and I felt a sense of peace. This time it was Pete who opened his heart to me; it was he who offered me that healing space of harmony that I so needed.

Thank you, Pete, for teaching me that it is when we touch each other's hearts with compassion that we find true healing.

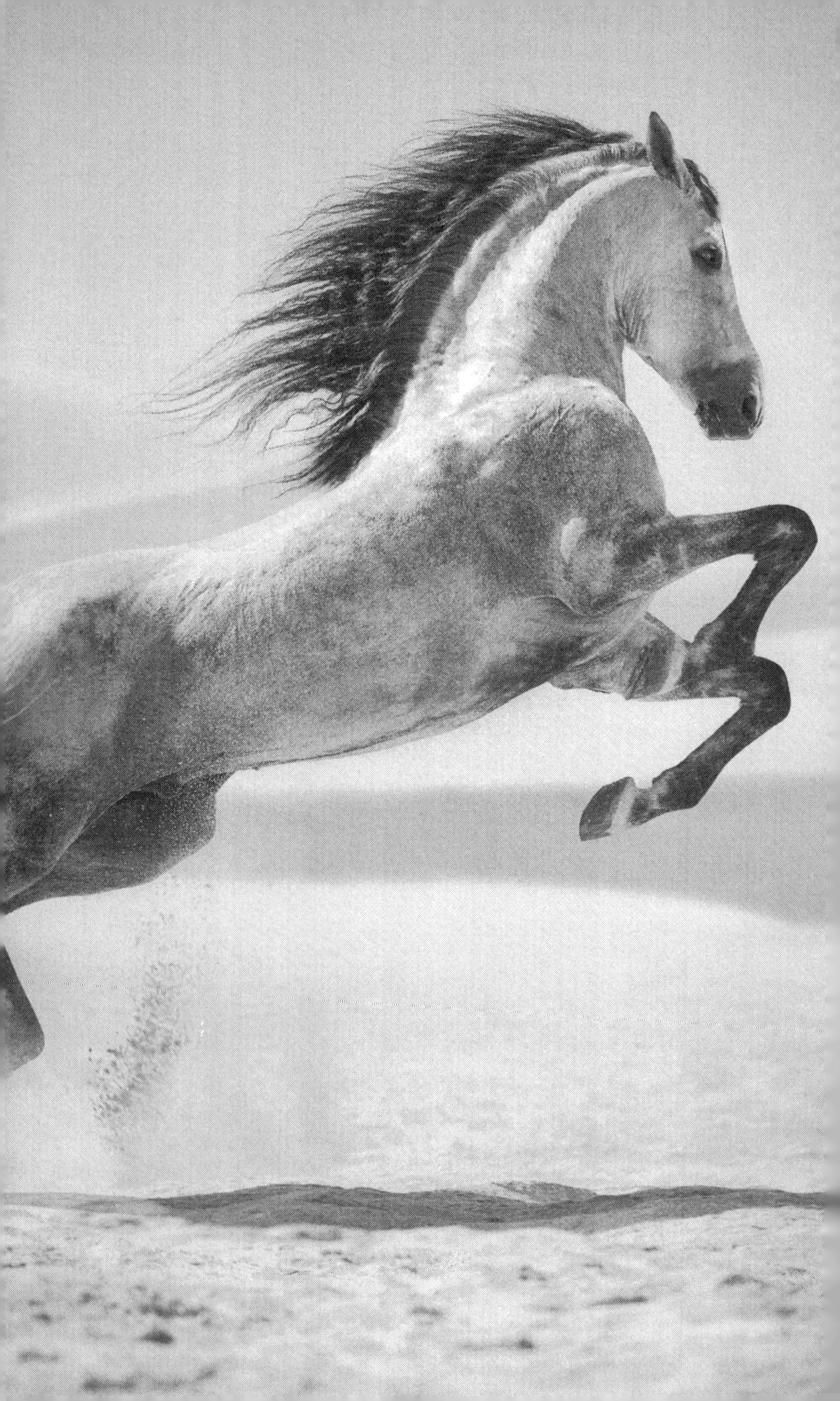

# Spirit Horse Meditation

Find a comfortable position in which to sit. Relax your shoulders and arms. Relax your body and legs. Close your eyes and take a couple of deep breaths into your belly.

Imagine that you are a wild horse, free to roam the earth. You are a physical body, and yet you are much more. Your physical hooves stand stable upon the ground, and yet the energy from your hooves stretches deep into the earth. In fact, you *are* the earth. A gentle breeze blows your physical mane upwards from your neck, and yet your energetic mane reaches even farther, high into the sky. In fact, you *are* the sky. You graze in the shade of a lovely strong tree. You are wild, powerful, and strong, and yet at the same time you are peaceful and content, fully present in this moment. You can feel your fierceness, your courage, and the fiery energy of your vibrant heart—this is an ancient energy, deeply connected to the earth and full of wisdom and compassion and the expansiveness of the sky.

Becoming one with this spirit horse, you can remember how to access your inner strength from a stable and grounded place. Your equine wisdom can remember that in this moment, all healing possibility exists within you, and this will help you have the courage to face whatever healing issues you or your loved ones may face. Say yes to this sharing of energy with the spirit horse, yes to remembering your inner courage, yes to healing potential and possibility. Take a moment to feel your connection to the spirit horse, no separation between you—you are One.

Imagine that with the assistance of your spirit horse, the ancient wisdom of the earth can flow up through your hooves and into your heart, grounding and stabilizing you. Imagine your mane reaches up into the limitless universe. Feel the warm, healing light of compassion shining down on you—this is the expansive energy of the sky. Compassion can move down through your mane, into your crown, and throughout your body into your heart. Feel ancient wisdom moving up from the earth, and expansive compassion shining down from the sky, mixing within your heart. With the help of earth and sky, it is easy to deeply experience wisdom and compassion, which creates strength within you. You are stable and grounded. You can feel courage too, creating a beautiful bright light that spreads out from you as the spirit horse, expanding the healing gifts of wisdom and compassion out into the world around you. You are earth. You are sky. You are perfect balance. You are presence. You are courage. You are healing.

Now I'd like you to bring to your mind a companion horse in your life who is facing a healing challenge. See him or her standing next to your spirit horse of courage. Very gently invite him/her to share in the limitless healing power of ancient wisdom and expansive compassion—the gifts of the earth and the sky and the spirit horse. Feel the light of your spirit horse shining so brightly that all healing potential exists in this very moment. Healing for body, mind, and spirit is possible now. Feel the spirit horse helping you access your inner courage to be able to hold this healing space for your companion horse, no matter what the issues he or she must face. Feel courage radiating strongly within this peaceful space.

Relax into this peaceful, healing energy. Feel that this space is simply a state of being—there is nothing to do, nothing to fix, no worries or fear. Within this space you can simply surrender to the flow of the universe. Within this space the universe understands healing and balance at the ultimate level. Feel how easily this letting go can happen with the support of your spirit horse. Let go and simply be.

For several minutes, in your mind, recite these words: Peaceful mind, peaceful heart, peaceful body. Healed mind, healed heart, healed body.

Now take a moment to thank your companion horse for his/her openness to the healing space you created. Thank your spirit horse for helping you access your grounding and expansiveness and reminding you of your inner strength and courage. Remember that your spirit horse of healing wisdom and compassion is always there inside of you, whenever you need him.

When you are ready, take a nice, deep, cleansing breath, and slowly come back and open your eyes.

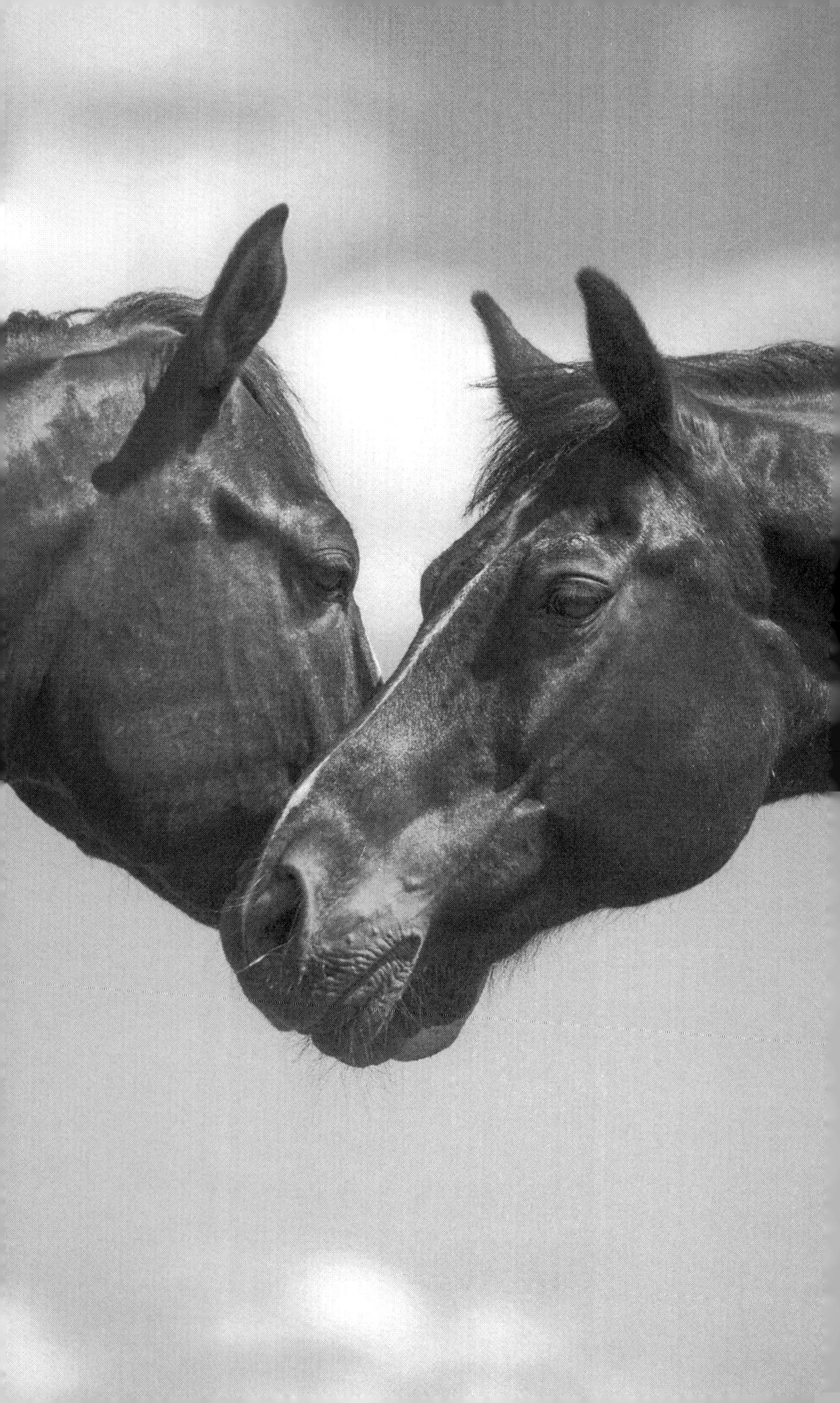

## CHAPTER 8
# Healing Fear and Finding Courage

*"I am an old man and have known a great many troubles. But most of them have never happened."*

—Mark Twain

I LOVE THIS QUOTE because it illustrates a great truth about worries: mostly, they never come true. So in reality, when we worry, we spend a lot of time and energy on negative thinking that isn't real. I find this very interesting because so often, we give ourselves a very hard time about imagining good or amazing possibilities in our lives. Like, we might say to ourselves, "Oh, well, that's unrealistic. That's just hoping for too much. I don't deserve that much happiness."

We should ask ourselves why it's so difficult to think affirmative thoughts. Sometimes we don't even let our minds entertain the awesome possibilities of the good things that could happen to us, like being completely joyful, or igniting our heart's or soul's passion, or discovering what brings us perfect peace—finding it and living it. Or maybe we have wished to find the perfect partner who brings out all of our best characteristics, but can't believe that we ever will. Maybe we want to live life with gusto and fearlessness all the way to old age, but something stops us.

Many of us find it very difficult to even allow ourselves to consider these kinds of amazing possibilities because we tell ourselves they are unlikely or impossible. On the other hand, it seems that we feel fine about spending hours ruminating on worries or obsessing about bad things that, most of the time, don't happen either.

So today, right now, I'm going to ask you to do something absolutely and totally crazy. I want you to start imagining awesome, beautiful, and healing possibilities in your life. I want you to imagine that these miraculous possibilities can happen everywhere you go and in everything you do.

Remember that everything we accomplish in our lives always starts with a thought. It has to start there before we can accomplish it. So let's start by turning our thoughts to the positive. I warn you that it's not going to be easy, because we've had so much practice in the other direction—the direction of worry. We've grown up visualizing negative scenarios, but that's okay. Please just give it a try. I'm suggesting to you today that there is something even stronger than your fear: love! The universe is so wide and so infinite. Why not open up your wings and fly? Don't wait. Do it today. Yes, it will take courage and yes, you're going to find a million reasons why not to test your wings. But in the words of writer Ambrose Redmoon, "Courage is not the absence of fear but rather the judgment that something else is more important than fear."

The love you have for your horse is more important than fear and will give you the strength to rise above the fear into the sky of infinite healing possibility! Opening yourself more fully to this loving relationship not only heals you both but also makes room for more love, and thus more healing, to flow into your life. Let's start now! Bring to your mind the horses you love most in this world. See them here with you. Feel them in your heart. They're here with you right now because of your love. It is for your beloved horses that you must learn to fly like Pegasus. The most beautiful gift you can give them is to allow them to see you in your full splendor of being *you*. In return, they will also share with you their most precious possessions: their heart and their presence.

> *"Being deeply loved by someone gives you strength, while loving someone deeply gives you courage."*
>
> —Lao Tzu

The love that you have for your horses, and the love they return to you—this is what will guide you to your courage. It's going to help you soar. It's going to help you to fly. It's going to help you to transform and become as wide and infinite as the universe. It will help you to learn the deeper meaning of the Reiki precept, "do not worry." It's so simple: love is going to show you the way. So when you feel lost or afraid, go back to your heart. Find that love and you will find your courage again.

I know this is true, because my horses have helped me to rediscover my own courage more than once. I know that your horses can help you to remember yours, too, if you let them. I shared earlier in this book about my paint, Kodiak, who helped me recover my joy in riding after my breast cancer surgery. He's quite a dominant and wild personality, and he has always been a handful since we first met.

I will always remember the first time I introduced him to my husband. My husband isn't much of a horse person, but he wanted to see the new "family member," and so he came out to the farm and waited by the barn for me to go get our new "baby." To get up to the barn, I had to cross a wooden bridge, and my husband was waiting on the other side. I was walking with Kodiak across the bridge, and something spooked him. He started cantering around me. So suddenly I was turning in circles with this crazy horse running wild.

I looked over at my husband and he was just shaking his head. I could see it written all over his face: "You're crazy! What is this monster that you have brought home to us?" There was nothing for me to do but helplessly hold the lead rope until Kodiak calmed down, which he did pretty quickly. Wow, *that* was a first impression!

Yes, Kodiak is one strong horse. But there has always just been something special about him. When I met him, I'd been looking for a horse for a long time—I just couldn't find one that spoke to me. I will always remember that day: I was standing with my trainer and a friend, just the three of us, when Kodiak's person brought him out to say hello. Kodiak walked straight up to us and put his nose right on my heart. Gently, he pushed me just a little bit, just a tiny little push into my heart. The lady said, "Well, he's never done that before. That's interesting."

He spoke to my heart in that moment, and my heart opened up and answered back. So there it was, our first Reiki conversation with each other. I knew he was the one. And you know, I think there was something in his wildness, the straightforwardness of his strength, that reminded me of something in myself: maybe a strength and a courage that I had yet to tap into.

A year later, I was blessed with pregnancy. Besides the fact that I was feeling too under the weather to visit my horses very often, Kodiak's strength and unpredictability served to keep us at a distance from each other; I had to have somebody else bring him out when I would go visit him. Even after I gave birth to my daughter, being a bit out of practice, I was a bit fearful of him, and he began to take advantage of that. Sometimes he would just run off when I was leading him. Most of the time it was just to graze, but there I was trailing after him like a rag doll dragging behind a steam engine. Horses are so intuitive, and although I loved him very much and tried to hide my fear, he could see right to the truth.

Over the years, I made a habit of avoiding this problem by only riding Kodiak. He was so perfect under saddle! I kept all my groundwork with him at a minimum because he was so strong and challenging. But through all of this time, there was a little voice inside me that told me he just wanted to play. Sometimes when I was walking next to Kodiak he would give me a look, and then he would shoulder-butt me before running off to graze. It was as if he was saying, "Na-na-na-na-na! Come and get me!" I was just too fearful to face this part of our relationship head on.

Well, this all began to change after I had breast cancer. Partly this was because cancer had set a new bar in my life for fear. I began to realize, "Hey, wait a minute! This horse is the favorite part of my day. How did I let fear sneak into this?" I understood that Kodiak acted up once in a while. Well, okay, sometimes he was a big brute. But compared to cancer, his antics were nothing. And besides, I really loved this horse! So very slowly, my courage began to show itself.

I thought of this quote by Mary Anne Radmacher: "Courage doesn't always roar. Sometimes courage is the little voice at the end of the day that says, 'I will try again tomorrow.'" So I did try, again and again, tomorrow and tomorrow and tomorrow and tomorrow. One day, I was finally ready to stand in my courage. I drew a line in the sand, and basically told Kodiak, "There's a new sheriff in town, and you can't cross this line. No, really, you can't cross it." No longer would I be the rag doll dragging behind the freight train; he was going to walk beside me, and politely, at that!

It wasn't easy. I had to stop and admit to myself, "Actually, I'm really afraid of this situation." But it takes a lot of the power of fear away when we actually just stop and look at it. This is when we begin to transform our fear because even just looking at it takes quite a bit of courage.

For a week or so, Kodiak kept giving me looks that said, "Mom, what's going on? Mom, is that you?" He tried all of his old tricks, and none of them worked. Then one day, something wonderful happened. My newfound courage allowed me to play with him. We were working on the lunge line, and I was standing in the center of a circle as he went around me and I asked him to walk, trot, canter, stop, and back up, doing all our little exercises. At one point, I asked him to canter again, and he suddenly got this funny look in his eye, as if to say, "Let's go!" He kicked up his heels and he bucked and he shook his head. He started to gallop around me, just going crazy.

Now, through all of this craziness, he didn't pull on the rope at all. So he was going a bit wild, but in a gentle way, just for me. I could see there was so much energy and so much bliss and joy in him. Before I got cancer, this burst of energy would have terrified me. I would have tried to stop him, or I would have called for help from someone. But this time, perhaps because of all the things that I had gone through in my own personal recovery, my courage was able to peek through.

At that moment, with Kodiak running wild circles around me, I got the biggest smile. I felt so still and grounded in the middle of his display, just like I was in the eye of a powerful storm. So I just smiled and let him gallop to his heart's content. He just kicked up his heels with more joy and exuberance than I had ever seen him display in all the years that I'd had him.

It was magical. When he got a bit tired, he slowed down to the most gigantic trot I had ever seen. He was just floating, and his eye was on me the whole time, as if he were saying, "Look what I can do, Mom!" I told him, "Wow, you're so beautiful!" He was so proud of his strength, and I could see that he just wanted to show me what he could do. It was as if he was saying to me, "Finally, Mom, I can be big! I can be my big self and you can stand in that space with me in your courage. So now we can truly be together."

After this big, crazy display, I rode him for a little bit, and it was one of the best rides I had ever had with him. As we were trotting together, he again got the big floating trot that I had seen from the ground. It felt amazing to be riding him and feeling so in unity with him. It was at that moment that I suddenly realized what had happened with him on the ground. We had just played! Tears of gratitude welled up within me, and I realized that finding my own courage had opened up a door to a new connection with Kodiak. Since that moment, he's been a different horse with me as I lead him. He listens, and he's respectful! And you know what else? I could already feel that newfound courage rippling out into other parts of my life. I know that it's going to keep expanding out for a long time to come.

It was enough to make me wonder: Without Kodiak challenging me, forcing me to face my fears and act with courage, could I have opened that door to my courage by myself? I don't know. I certainly couldn't have done it as easily without him as I did with him. Truly, our horses can help us to remember our inner courage better than any teacher I know! My experience with Kodiak also reminded me that it's always our most difficult teachers who teach us the biggest lessons. When we remember this, it becomes much easier to stay in a space of gratitude when we are facing difficulties.

So who are the horses in your life who are waiting to help you to release your fear and stand in your courage? Can you see them in your mind's eye right now? Let them in. Let them show you how to face your fears, and then *release* those fears. As we learn to stand in our courage, we learn how to be ourselves. We learn how to really *be* who we are, authentically and without apology. For example, in my relationship with Kodiak, I don't have to be strong and big the way he can be. I can still be my mild-mannered, quiet, small self. That's who I am. But when I remember my inner courage, it is possible for me to also hold the space for *him* to be who *he* is in all his bigness and exuberance.

When we stand in our courage, no one else can take away from whom we are, and it becomes easier to let others be who they are as well. When we're afraid to be who *we* are, our animals don't feel safe to be who *they* are. Once we learn to *be honest*, as the Reiki precept reminds us, everything else just seems to begin to flow so much more freely. As Samuel Johnson said, "Courage is the greatest of all the virtues because if you haven't courage, you may not have an opportunity to use any of the others."

Courage often is the key that opens the door to so many possibilities in life. If we can learn to focus on letting go of fear and opening ourselves to courage, the flow of the universe will just take over and we can fly into the stars of our potential just like Pegasus. Our horses can help us to do that.

## Case Study: *Reiki for Joe*
## by Sally Long

When I met Joe, he was a beautiful, warm-blooded ten-year-old horse who was emotionally shut down, head-shaking whenever he was stressed and experiencing severe separation anxiety whenever he was away from his herd. He had physical problems too, such as arthritis in his back quarters and mud fever on his legs.

Joe was scared when asked to do anything, such as being led in and out of the yard or through a gate. He was not unkind, but he was extremely apprehensive. I knew that in order to share Reiki with him, I would have to be very calm and grounded. I was careful not to ask him to "do" Reiki; instead I let Joe take the lead. Sometimes, of his own choice, he would walk over to me and stand just right so I could to place my hands on his neck. I could feel our hearts connect and he would start to drop his head, chew, and yawn. Sometimes he would move forward so my hands were resting on his hind end, and other times he would lean his forehead on me; he always showed me just where he wanted to be touched.

After several sessions I began to notice subtle changes in Joe's behavior; the deeper our bond through Reiki, the calmer and more responsive he became. With the love and trust Reiki created, in time Joe was able to let go of fear. Amazingly, he improved physically, as well as becoming a very confident, happy horse.

## Case Study: *Buddy Lets Go of Fear*
### by Michele Rodriguez

Buddy and I found each other at the right time in both our lives. He was adopted in 2002, when he was six years old; he had been abused and malnourished. His adopter had worked with five trainers over the years, to no avail. Buddy was still a very unfriendly soul. He and his person were fine together, but only as long as no one else was around. As the old saying goes, there are no coincidences, and I was asked to come and provide Reiki to help. I thought I was there to help Buddy, but in reality I had found this troubled soul so I could also learn a lesson.

My first visit did not go very well. As I approached Buddy and his person, he began to snort, grunt, and stomp with his ears pinned down. He was not having any part of me. With the help of Reiki, I stood there creating a sacred space for both of us and envisioning peace for him. Although that day Buddy clearly said no to Reiki, I made an offer to his person to try coming back on a volunteer basis. Little did I know what an incredible lesson I would learn!

On my second visit, I walked up to the paddock where Buddy was and again, he began his unfriendly, unhappy behavior. With the help of Reiki, I focused on just bringing peace to the space. Buddy walked out of his stall and galloped to the far end of the paddock, where he stood stock still. I again envisioned a peaceful place for him. I thanked him for his beautiful presence. No matter what, Buddy was still beautiful to me.

My third visit was different. I sat outside the stall just speaking to Buddy, even humming a little. I noticed he was not upset. I walked inside the stall next to him and he walked, not galloped, out to the paddock. Again, I simply focused on peace. He stayed at the far end of the paddock. I positioned myself halfway between Buddy and the barn. Finally, amazingly, he turned around and stared at me. I closed my eyes, feeling his attention and presence and enjoying the beautiful day. We had made a connection! At the end of the session he galloped right past me into his stall, as if to say that he liked what he was feeling. I knew that for a short time Buddy had felt at peace. My eyes filled with tears as I realized we had connected on a deeper level. As I left, he looked at me with such peace in his heart. I thanked him for such a moving experience.

On my fourth visit, Buddy watched me from the moment I closed my car door. I sat in front of his stall and he looked at me, and even hung his head over the gate. Oh, he so badly wanted to be touched! I petted him, and he did not back away. I went out to the paddock while he walked around watching me. As I began my Reiki meditation, Buddy walked right up to my hands! I knew this was the first time that he had let a stranger get close to him. He trusted the Reiki connection, and me.

Buddy taught me that fear can always be healed. Courage can be built with patience and gentle presence without expectation.

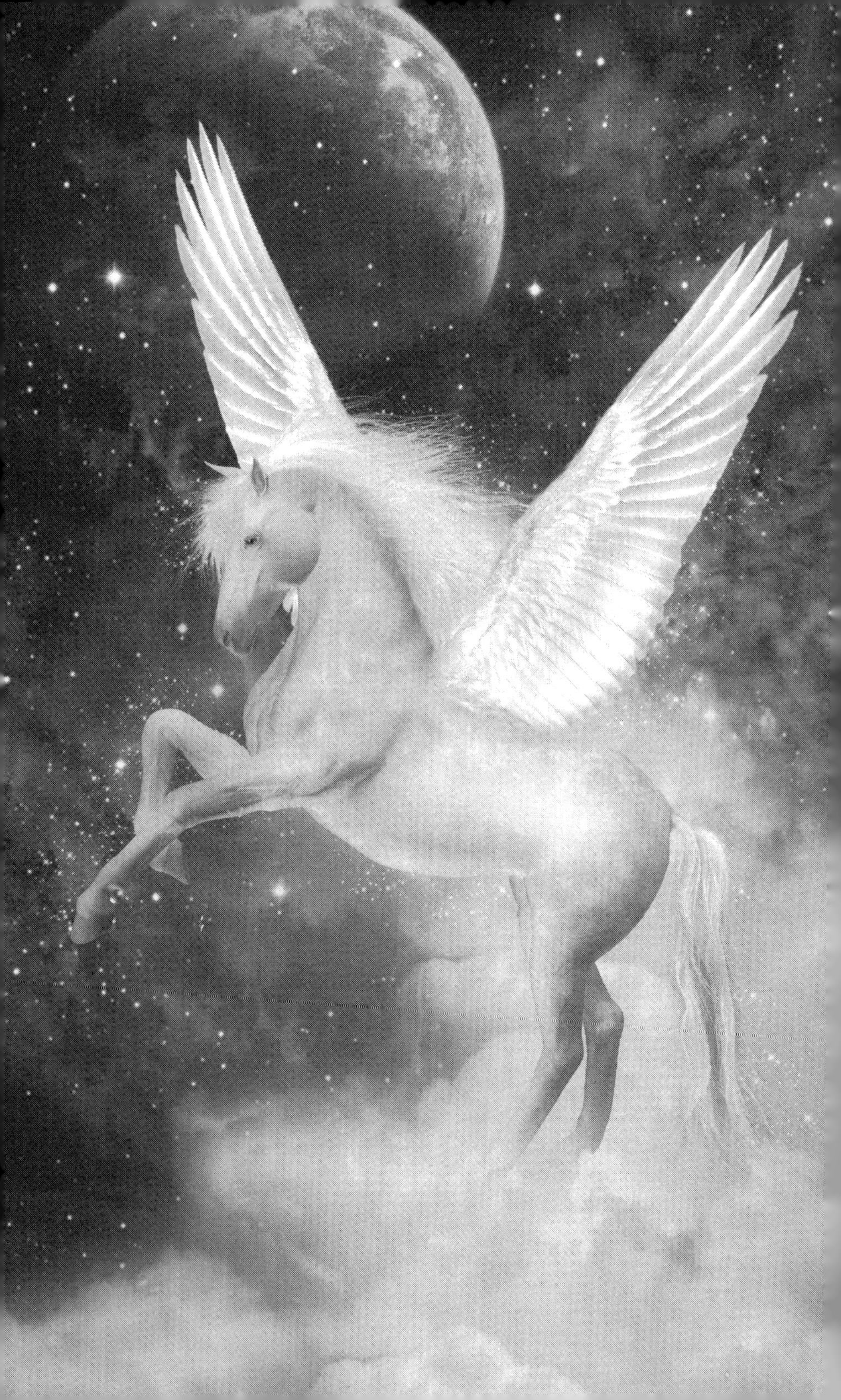

## Pegasus and Courage Meditation

One of childhood's most iconic mythic creatures is the Pegasus, the winged horse. A horse that can fly is a wonderful symbol of infinite strength, courage, and potential. Pegasus also helps us remember the Reiki precept, "Do not worry." In this meditation, let's take a journey to courage through finding our inner Pegasus.

Find a comfortable position in which to sit; relax your body and your arms, your shoulders and your legs. Place your hands on your lap, palms up or palms down, whatever is most comfortable.

Hold your spine nice and straight so energy can flow easily through your spine and through your whole body. Close your eyes and take a nice, deep, cleansing breath and let it out slowly. Take another nice, deep breath and let it out slowly.

Feel yourself relaxing with each breath, letting go of all of the stresses from your day and just being here right now in this present moment. Now, I'm going to take you on a little journey. Imagine that you're sitting on a bench in a beautiful garden surrounded by hundreds of flowers. Look around you and see the flowers: red and yellow, purple and pink, blue and white—big flowers, little flowers, short flowers and trailing flowers, all kinds of flowers all around you.

Allow yourself to close your eyes and inhale the wonderful floral scent that fills the air. Suddenly, a winged horse appears in front of you. Slowly raise your hand and touch his nose. Gaze at his powerful wings of white feathers. As you stare deeper into the bright white of his massive wings, you can feel everything else beginning to fall away. As his wings begin to move, white is all around you and even within your heart; it is as if your heart beats in sync with the beat of the Pegasus's wings.

Pegasus symbolizes letting go of our fears by rising above them, harnessing our inner power so we can fly to new heights.

When we let go of our fears and worries, we open a new space in our lives where joy and bliss can come in and heal us. Pegasus says, "Don't be afraid to open your wings and fly wherever your heart takes you!" Pegasus reminds us to never limit ourselves. Follow your passion, follow your bliss, for when you do, you will make the universe a beautiful place.

Relax into a connection with the Pegasus. Be One. Suddenly you find yourself transformed, flying high above the earth, in the clouds. Notice the shapes of all the clouds beneath you and around you. These clouds begin to transform themselves into the shapes and shadows of your life. With the power and strength of the Pegasus, you can safely visit different places and times in your life. First, find a place where you allow fear to rule you. See yourself there, in that small dark place of fear. You are there only because you are unaware of the bright light just beyond the limits which fear has put upon you. Show yourself compassion and love. Know that you always do the very best that you can at each moment. But now, with the power of the Pegasus, imagine that you can rise above it all with your powerful wings and transform these places of fear in your life into courage.

Allow yourself to really see these situations of fear in your life. Let your winged horse dissolve the fear. Let Pegasus reawaken the courage within you so that you can embrace healing, joy, and bliss. Whatever the situation, the attitude, the relationship, the path, whatever it is that you see fear ruling, imagine yourself drawing a line in the sand. Fear will no longer rule. You can transform this situation easily if you bring courage into your mind and heart. Know that if you can imagine it, you can do it.

Clearly and completely see yourself acting with courage in this situation. What does this look like? How does manifesting your courage heal the situation? Take a moment to see that healing happen. Allow yourself. Give yourself permission. Bring forth courage and transform fear right now.

As your dark cloud of fear leaves you and melts away, feel yourself emerging into the light, flying with the strong wings of Pegasus. Feel yourself so white, light, and open that no darkness, no fear can stick to you. You are utterly bright like the sun; let yourself fly high up into the sky and embrace your bliss. Take a few moments to enjoy this beautiful, healing gift from your winged Pegasus. Feel that bliss starting in your heart, rippling out into your physical body, your emotional body, your mental body, your spiritual body. The strength and courage of Pegasus is yours. Healing potential is yours right now. Embrace it.

Take a moment to thank your Pegasus for sharing his amazing power with you.

Now return to the garden of beautiful flowers. Pegasus brings you back to the bench where you began this journey. Feel yourself transforming back into your human form. Feel the earth beneath your feet. You are grounded and centered.

Remember that your inner Pegasus represents the courage you already have inside of you. You always have the power to transform fear into courage; you only need to remember it. Set your intention to finish, and take a nice, deep, cleansing breath and slowly come back and open your eyes.

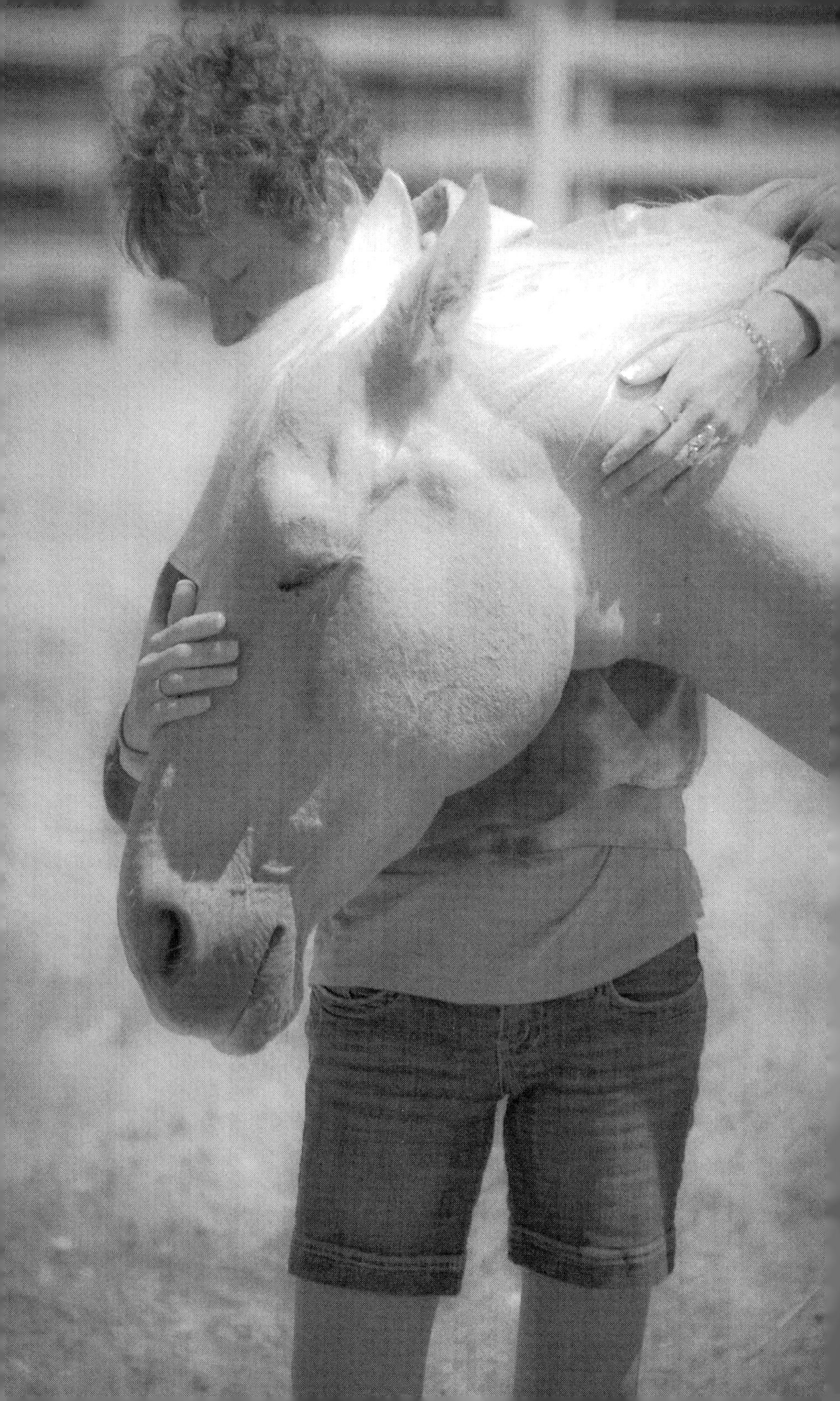

## CHAPTER 9
# Ways to Meditate

*"In meditation, effort must be applied in a direction opposite to what we are used to. Our 'effort' must be to relax ever more deeply. We must ultimately release the tension from both our muscles and our thoughts. When we relax so deeply that we are able to internalize the energy of the senses, the mind becomes focused and a tremendous flow of energy is awakened.... . Meditation is a continuous process, and can be said to have three stages: relaxation, interiorization, and expansion."*

—John Novak, *Lessons in Meditation*

AS YOU HAVE read throughout this book so far, Reiki is a meditative practice. So in a nutshell, when you share Reiki with a horse, what this means is that you are going to be meditating with the horse, and inviting him/her into the healing atmosphere created by the meditation.

The system of Reiki offers very simple practices to help us to remember that we are all connected in this web of life. Sharing Reiki with animals makes this truth even more self-evident, as all species differences can melt away in the space of a Reiki session.

The most important benefit of Reiki is that it nurtures compassion: compassion within ourselves for our own healing, and compassion for the support of others. People who practice Reiki often describe how their meditation practice has helped them connect heart to heart and has changed their lives from the inside out, helped their animals, and even made their world a better and more peaceful, compassionate place.

Sharing Reiki with horses means that you will be able to practice meditation in many different ways. While in the beginning you may find it easiest to meditate sitting still with your eyes closed, your horses will challenge you to learn how to meditate while standing and walking with your eyes open. This is because horses already understand that true meditation isn't so much about your physical position as it is simply about being mindful in this present moment.

Spending time with our horses during meditation can help us to develop our own sensitivities and awareness. Animals are wonderful models for us since they already embody a purity and authenticity of *being* that we as humans must practice and strive to achieve. Meditation with our horses can help guide us to a life of being better people and creating a healthier planet, one where people nurture wellness through the practice of compassion and service to others.

Most of the meditations taught so far in this book are best used while alone at home (envisioning your horse in your mind), when sitting outside the paddock or while standing quietly with your horse, but it's also possible to meditate while walking or riding! Here are some suggestions to help you branch out and try some new and creative approaches to sharing Reiki with your horse!

## *Four great ways to meditate with your horse*

1. Sitting Meditation: For this type of meditation, sit outside the stall or paddock where your horse lives. You can choose to play your favorite music while wearing earbuds to help you to relax; you can also choose to just listen to and enjoy the wonderful sounds of horses around you. The sounds of horses grazing or ambling through tall grass are music to my ears!

### Sun/Moon Sitting Meditation:

Sit with your horse, but for safety, just outside the pasture or stall. Sit on the ground or on a stool or chair, close your eyes, and rest your hands palms up on your lap. Set your intention that you dedicate this meditation to your horse. Take several deep breaths into your belly to ground yourself.

Imagine there is a glowing moon below your left foot, and a bright sun below your right foot. Say to yourself, "May my steps be always guided by wisdom and compassion."

Imagine another moon in your left hand, another sun in your right hand. Say to yourself, "May my actions be always guided by wisdom and compassion."

Relax into the connection with the sun and moon for several minutes.

When you are ready, slowly imagine that the suns and moons travel from your feet and hands to your heart, where they unify in a beautiful bright light. This is a space of pure wisdom and compassion where all healing is possible. Invite your horse to share that space with you.

If your horse comes close to you, place your hands on him gently, and feel the light of healing encompass you both.

2. Standing Meditation: For this meditation, stand inside or outside your horse's stall or paddock, or out in the pasture with the herd. My favorite place to do this type of meditation is out in nature with the horses, birds and squirrels, and with the sun, wind and earth under my feet to support the beautiful, peaceful space.

## Metta Practice with Horses (can be modified for any and/or all species)

Put your hands palms together in front of your heart and speak these words in your mind and heart as you share this space with your horses:

To yourself:

May I be joyful and peaceful.
May I be healthy, comfortable, and safe.
May I be in harmony with all things.

To your horse (or herd):

May you be joyful and peaceful.
May you be healthy, comfortable, and safe.
May you be in harmony with all things.

To all domesticated horses on the earth:

May you be joyful and peaceful.

May you be healthy, comfortable, and safe.

May you be in harmony with all things.

To all wild horses on the earth:

May you be joyful and peaceful.

May you be healthy, comfortable, and safe.

May you be in harmony with all things.

To all humans on earth:

May your heart open to the wisdom and compassion

Of being kind and gentle to yourself,

and also may you treat all horses with this same respect and gentleness.

Rest your hands at your sides and stay with your horses for as long as you like. Imagine these words can radiate healing and love out infinitely into the universe. If your horses approach you, gently rest your hands on them wherever they show you to touch. There is no need to move your hands to different positions, your horse will move their position relative to yours if they wish a different position; or they will move away if they prefer to connect from a distance.

3. Walking Meditation: This meditation is fun to do while hand-walking your horse somewhere where they like to graze. Imagine you and your horse are connected by your hearts, not by the lead rope. In this meditation, as

with the previous one, allow the natural environment around you to support you. Open yourself to the present moment in all its natural beauty.

*"The earth is sacred and we touch her with each step. We should be very respectful, because we are walking on our mother. If we walk like that, then every step will be grounding, every step will be nourishing."*

—Thich Nhat Hanh

## Walking Meditation with your Horse

Put your horse on a lead rope and find a quiet place to walk where you won't be disturbed—it could be a trail through the woods, a country road near the barn, or even just the arena on the property where your horse lives.

As you breathe in, count how many steps your horse takes; as you breathe out, count your horse's steps. Breathe in and out, counting your horse's steps in this way for several minutes. Make sure to keep your breath relaxed, just allow it to naturally rise and fall with the steps of your horse. Then begin to notice the pace of your own steps in relation to your horse's. Feel your connection to your horse through each step, through each breath and through your heart.

You can continue to walk together, or choose to let your horse graze, while you speak the following affirmations in your mind:

(inhale) "I am the earth."

(exhale) "The earth is in me."

(inhale) "My horse (name) is the earth."

(exhale) "The earth is in my horse."

(inhale and exhale) "Each step forward together manifests our peace, love, and joyful connection."

Take your time with this, repeating it as many times as you like. Then simply walk in silence and with an open heart with your horse. If your horse is open to it, rest one hand on his neck or mane as you walk. If he stops to graze, stand beside him and, if he is open to it, rest a hand on his shoulder. Continue to feel your grounding from the earth and your hearts as One.

4. Riding Meditation: The following sphere meditations are best done in one of two ways. If you have a friend who can lead your horse while you ride, you can fully go into the meditation. If you have a very calm horse, you can practice these meditations while walking in a familiar spot that is quiet—perhaps your arena. Keep your eyes and awareness open.

# The Four Spheres Riding Meditation

**Hara Sphere:** Grounding and Peace

As you ride your horse at the walk, imagine your *hara* (the energy center in your lower belly) is a bright sphere filled with earth energy: grounded, calm, powerful. Slowly expand this sphere to encompass your entire body. Then imagine you can slowly expand it to encompass both you and your horse. Invite your horse to connect with you in this grounded calm and peaceful space. Relax and just feel the movement of the horse, be aware of your connection to the earth through your horse's footsteps.

**Heart Sphere:** Love and Compassion

As you ride your horse at the walk, imagine your heart is a bright sphere filled with compassion and love energy. Slowly expand this sphere to encompass your entire body. Then slowly expand it to encompass both you and your horse.

Invite your horse to connect with you in this compassionate harmonious space, without judgment, without expectation. Relax and just feel the movement of the horse, be aware of your connection to your horse at the heart.

**Mind Sphere:** Openness and Harmony

As you ride your horse at the walk, imagine at your forehead is a bright sphere filled with peace and harmony. Imagine you can let go of your thoughts and allow peace to fill your mind. Slowly expand this sphere to encompass your entire body. Then expand it to encompass both you and your horse. Invite your horse to connect with you in this quiet and open space. Relax and just feel the movement of the horse, feel his awareness of you as you become more and more relaxed, feel your horse also relaxing. Be aware of your connection to each other in this open mind space.

**Hands Sphere:** Performing Gratitude and Devotion for your Horse

As you ride your horse at the walk, imagine at each hand is a bright sphere filled with gratitude and devotion. Slowly expand these spheres to encompass your entire body. Then slowly expand them to encompass both you and your horse. Invite your horse to connect with you in this graceful space of gratitude and devotion for each other. Rest your hands on your horse's shoulders, relax and feel your movement in sync with your horse, and imagine that your hands are simply extensions of your heart. Your hands will always do the heart's work of devotion for your horse. Your hands will always move with gratitude and respect for your horse.

# Case Study: *Donkeys Love Reiki Too!*
# by Ann Noyce

> *"To be trusted is a greater compliment than being loved."*
>
> —George MacDonald

A sweet donkey named Frankie gave me the compliment of trust one bright, sunny spring afternoon at Holyland Donkey Haven near Fond du Lac, Wisconsin.

A few of my students and I met at the sanctuary for an afternoon of Reiki with the donkeys. As we met and said hello to the donkeys, Frankie was clearly not comfortable interacting with us. In fact, Frankie was fairly new and had not yet been able to settle in at the sanctuary.

We spread out in the paddock Frankie shares with five or six other donkeys. We created a healing circle of Reiki meditation and invited the donkeys to join us. The donkeys moved around the paddock, grazing. A couple of them took turns coming forward to stand in front of us; some grazed behind us. Even the donkeys in the next paddock came over by the fence to be closer to us. We let the donkeys move around and experience the energy as they wished.

At one point, I felt a sense of warmth and looked up. Frankie was standing there, across the paddock, looking at me very intently. Everyone noticed how Frankie was focused on me. I looked back at Frankie and we shared a beautiful one-on-one connection for a few minutes. After this one treatment, there was an immediate shift in his behavior: Frankie was finally able to find calm and peace and settle into his new home at the sanctuary.

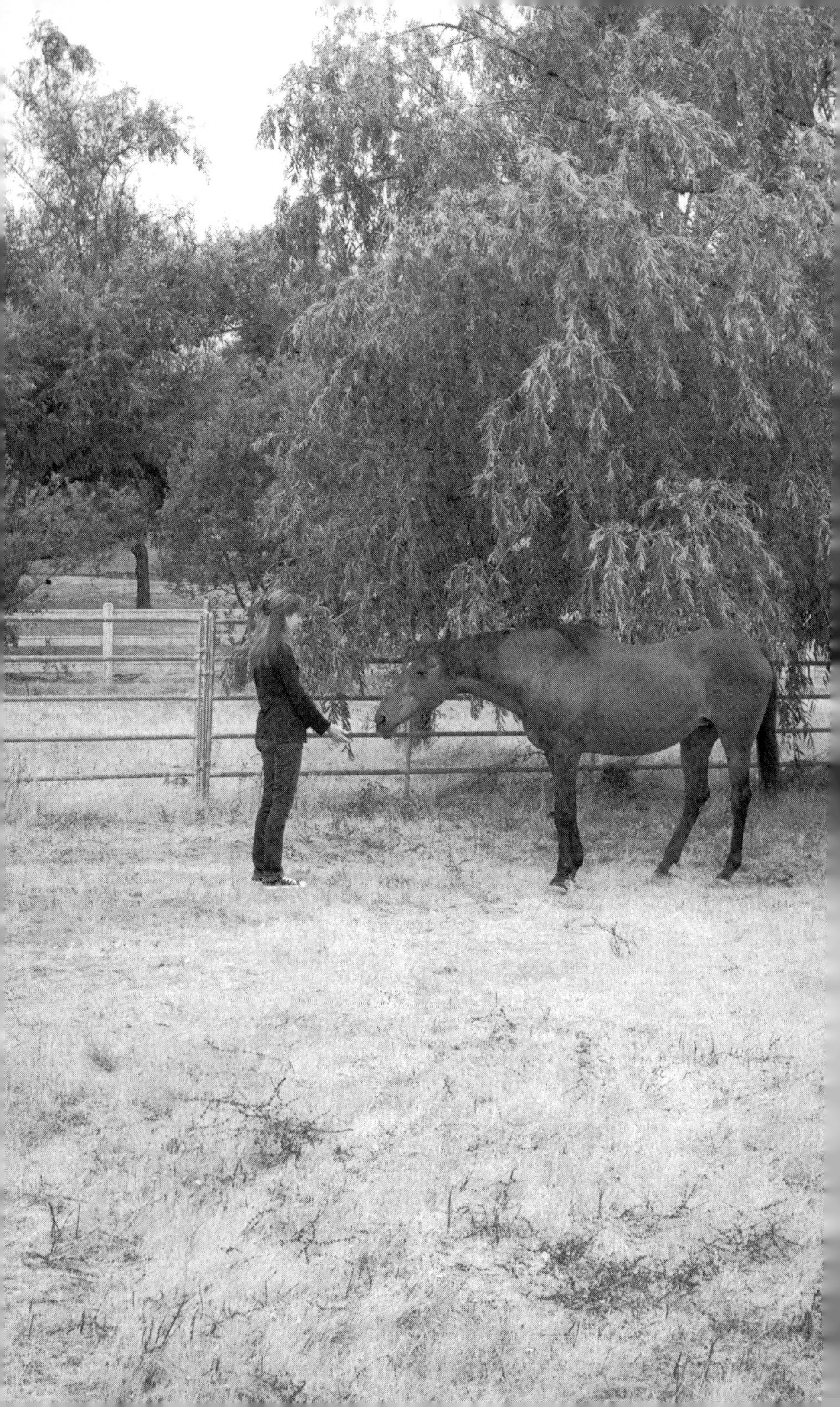

## CHAPTER 10
# Heart to Heart Connections

*"To understand the horse you'll find that you're going to have to work on yourself. This is life, this is reality, there is no rulebook on this and it's damn hard to grasp because it comes from deep down inside. I've been trying my whole life, and I'm still working at it. I hope you get there before me, 'cause then you can help me out. But I owe it to the horse to work this hard."*

—Ray Hunt

THE MOST IMPORTANT thing for us to do, if we want to be able to share effective and powerful Reiki sessions with our horses, in other words, if we want to share heart-to-heart connections with them, is to create a daily meditation practice. This isn't easy, and in fact takes a lot of discipline. But your horses are worth it! Even if at first it is only five minutes two times a day, that is a great start in training ourselves in mindfulness. And you will see in time that the peaceful centeredness that Reiki creates during your meditation will begin to ripple out into other areas of your life. The best proof for you that your Reiki practice with your horses is working will be your own remarkable self-transformation!

Now that we've discussed what Reiki meditation is, how it can bring peace and healing to both you and your horses, and some meditation exercises that you can do both in your home and in the company of your horses, I'd like to discuss some techniques that can enhance our ability to connect heart-to-heart with the horses we love.

## *Mirroring*

Always use mirroring when moving during a Reiki session. Mirroring our horse's movements when we are sharing Reiki creates a beautiful dancelike synchrony; it also trains our observation skills. Mirroring shows our horses that they can trust us because we are paying attention to what they are telling us. Mirroring helps us practice letting the horses' movements lead the way. To mirror your horse's movements, observe him carefully. When your horse moves away, take a step or two back. When your horse moves toward you, step forward. If your horse steps close enough for you to rest your hands on him, do so gently. Allow your horse to move under your hands, repositioning himself as is most comfortable for him. When your horse steps away, drop your hands and take a step back.

In the beginning, we are mirroring only the physical movements of the horses, but in time and with more practice, we can learn to go deeper and read the energy of our horse. This takes lots of time and practice, first focusing on outer movements. Soon we learn to look deeper and sense whether we should move towards our horses, perhaps rest our hands on them, or step away from them simply by reading their energy. Again, this is an exercise in letting our horses' energy lead us. It's also a way to learn how to connect from the heart.

## *Horses as guides*

It's important to remember when sharing Reiki with horses that the healing goes both ways. If we always focus on what we as humans are bringing to the horses, we will miss a very important component of heart to heart connection: the gifts the horses bring to us! Horses can reflect back to us our own healing strengths and challenges. For example, there may be certain horse personalities and healing issues that we may feel more kinship with, and others that make us very uncomfortable. Pay attention to these feelings inside yourself when you are with horses, as they will tell you a lot about yourself and what you need to be working on in your own life.

Horses are also lights along our journey. There may be days that we feel our path is so dark that we don't know which way to go. It is then that our horses might shine their lights and encourage us with the love and joy they radiate so effortlessly. If we take the time to open our hearts and listen, it becomes easy to follow their lead in the journey of healing—not just during a Reiki session, but in life.

## *The typical session*

There is a key difference in sharing Reiki with horses rather than people. People usually need the ritual of movement and touch to help them to connect with the meditative space. In a typical human-to-human Reiki session, the client will lie down on a massage table so the practitioner can perform a ritual set of hand positions on or near the body.

Horses, on the other hand, prefer to go straight to a much deeper place, connecting mind to mind or heart to heart. It is best for the practitioner to remain quiet and meditative, while holding an open mind. The physical ritual of hand positions and the overt nature of physical touch can disturb some horses, especially if they are sensitive. Horse Reiki sessions are most successful when the practitioner has developed his meditative skills enough that he can drop the physical ritual and simply offer an open heart and open state of mind, without judgment or expectation.

When a practitioner can quietly hold this kind of space, the horse may then move around the person, sometimes coming forward to receive hands-on contact, sometimes moving away. In the case of mirroring movements, it is the horse who usually leads.

Horses are so aware of energy and connections, they will happily take charge of their own Reiki sessions when we let them. Their deeper knowledge and awareness of energy guides us. If we learn to open our minds and hearts, our horses will show us just what to do, or more to the point, how to *be*.

After a lot of work with *hara* breathing, that develops our grounding, and also a lot of practice with looking deeper (seeing with our Reiki eyes)—and always with a spirit of humility—sometimes advanced practitioners are able to ask a horse if we may lead this mirroring game. When working with a stressed and hyperactive horse, we may make calm, slow movements, moving our hands downward towards the earth, feeling ourselves gather our energy towards the earth, into the earth. This can remind the horse how to remember peace and grounding. In this way, advanced practitioners can model for the unbalanced horse how to balance, center, and become calm. Remember though, that even when leading a mirroring type of session, always ask, don't tell. *Always model from a place of humility*—don't try to force something because you think you know "best."

## *Healing through shared Reiki sessions*

Sharing Reiki with horses is a wonderful way to connect for healing. For me, the teachings of Reiki are about opening our hearts and being truly present in a compassionate way for others. I think our horses already know that this is true healing, but for humans it is more difficult to realize. We often get distracted by the physical, wanting to "cure" this or that problem. We might begin to mistake Reiki's tools—the hand positions, the breathing techniques, the symbols and mantras, and so on—as ways to "fix" the things that worry or displease us. It is good to remember that the real power of the system of Reiki is to help us to be open-hearted and compassionate, for this is the ultimate healing—for ourselves, for the ones we love, and for the planet! Although sometimes it is difficult for us to independently open the doors to our inner awareness and understanding of the amazing power of compassion, I find that horses can open these doors for us very easily. They can teach us about compassion in the most life-transforming ways. Isn't that beautiful!

When we share Reiki, connecting with our horses, the healing goes two ways (or three, or four, or a hundred, depending on how many animals are taking part with us). Healing can happen for all of us who choose to share in this beautiful heart space. Reiki helps us open our hearts and radiate compassion, and the horses in this space will benefit from our positive radiance. In turn, when we choose to open our hearts in this receptive way, we are able to receive boundless peace, kindness, wisdom and healing gifts from the horses who come forward to connect with us. Reiki is a shared state of *being*, rather than an active state of doing. Oneness, compassion and healing: this is the space of Reiki.

# Case Study: *Hidalgo*
# by Monique MacMillan

I was pursuing an Animal Reiki internship with Kathleen and needed volunteer animals for my practices. My friend Carly agreed to a session with her beautiful registered paint gelding Hidalgo, aka HD. It just so happened that the weekend HD was going to have his first Reiki session, he injured his front left shoulder and was indoors for a few days to help his recovery. I offered to do four consecutive sessions to help kick-start the healing process, and Carly readily agreed.

Each session was memorable, but it was the last one that was the most valuable. HD stood about ten feet away from me, next to Carly. He stood there, very relaxed, and just enjoyed the Reiki space. His head was low and his eyes were very heavy. Occasionally, he swished his tail or moved his head to shoo away bugs, and from time to time, he lifted one hind leg and then the other. The session lasted an hour, and HD stood in that position during the whole session. It wasn't until I ended the session that HD moved; he walked up to me and smelled my hands. I thanked him for sharing the Reiki space and then said goodbye, and when I walked away, he followed me to the gate of the arena just like he does with Carly.

Even though I never placed my hands on HD during the session, he showed many signs of acceptance of Reiki. He taught me that hands weren't necessary for a successful sharing of Reiki, and that all I needed to do was hold the healing space through meditation and being present in the moment. Afterward, Carly confirmed that Reiki helped speed up HD's recovery and that he was relaxed after each session, even after being inside for a couple of days. Thank you, HD, for being such a wonderful teacher. It was a real honor to share the Reiki space with you.

# Case Study: *The Tree Meditation with Pepsi*
# by Caroline Thomas

It was a beautiful sunny September day at Remus Horse Sanctuary in Essex, England, and Kathleen was teaching her Equine Reiki class. Part of the day was spent in the Remus classroom, and the rest of the time was spent with the horses. Visualization or imagery has always been very difficult for me, so when Kathleen assigned us a Reiki meditation, I went and found a tree in the furthest part of the field. Not only did this beautiful tree give me shade, I also felt its grounding energy supporting me in this exercise. Feeling grounded and strong, I stood quietly until I saw from the corner of my eye a Black Shetland pony called Pepsi slowly moving towards me. Like a tree swaying in the wind, with each step Pepsi took towards me, I took a step towards him. With each step he backed away, I took a backward step. We were mirroring each other to a point we were almost dancing under the cool, strong oak tree. We both stopped when our steps brought us exactly face-to-face, only centimeters apart. Being connected to the earth and sky energy, feeling strength from the tree, I was able to hold a peaceful, compassionate space within my own heart and mind for Pepsi. After about twenty minutes, Pepsi walked back to the herd, and I felt so grateful for what I had just experienced. It was true heart to heart connection!

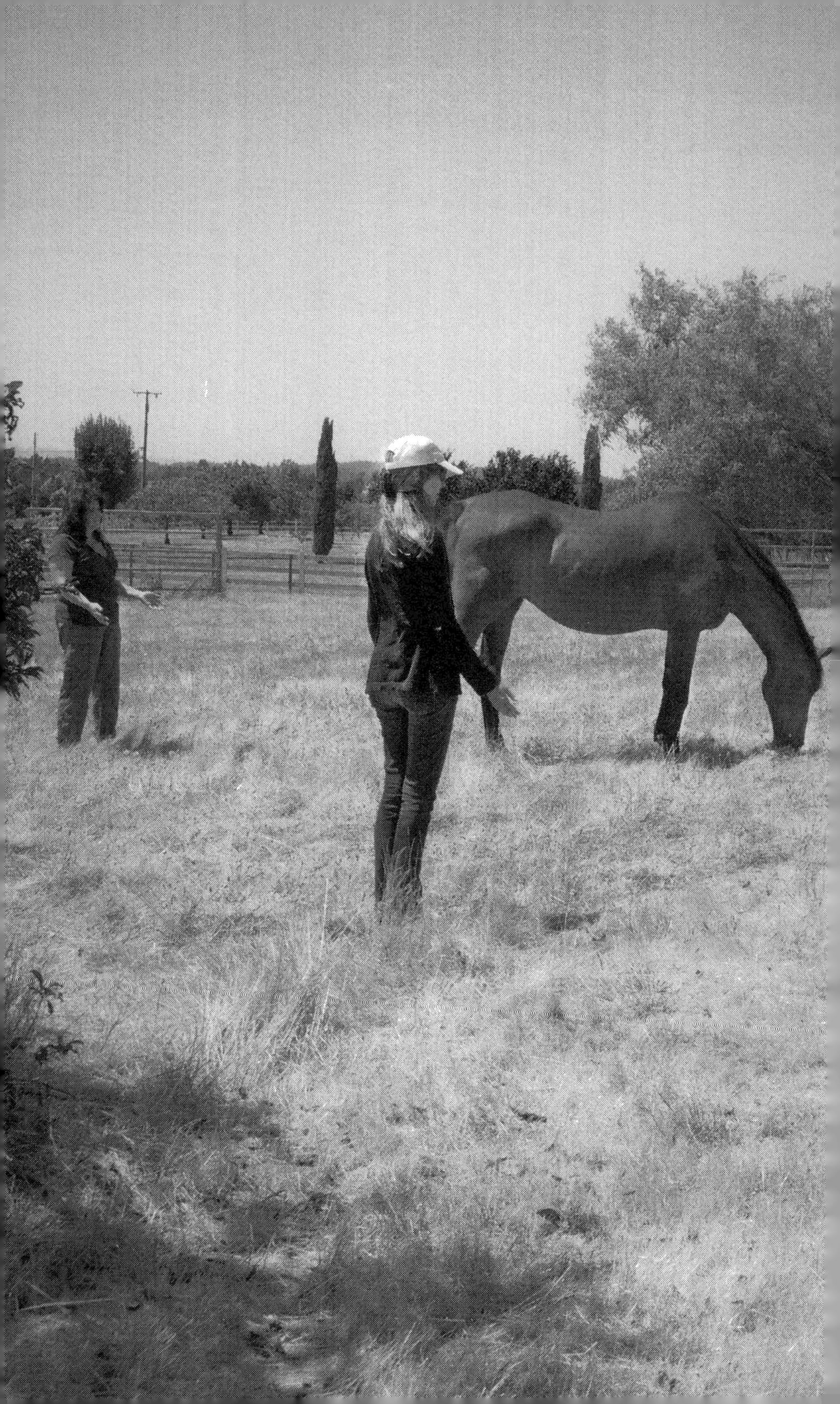

# CHAPTER 11
# Guidelines for Sharing Reiki with Your Horse

*It's got to come from here [your heart]. People are working on their horse; their horse is all right, [your heart] has got to get in order."*

—Ray Hunt

AS I HAVE emphasized in the last chapter, your state of heart and mind is the real key if you want to share Reiki successfully with your horses. I've created a short summary of best practices and safety tips to remember when you are ready to share Reiki.

## *Ethics*

In respect of your horse's wisdom, and to ensure a compassionate session, there are three essential ethical points you must remember every time you seek to share Reiki with your horses:

- *Reiki is a complementary therapy.* Reiki is not a replacement for veterinary care, but rather a wonderful complement to all other treatments. I often tell people to exchange the word *compassion* or *love* for the word Reiki. If you would offer compassion in a given situation, or love in that moment, then it's a great time for Reiki. If your horse is open, go for it!

- *Reiki is not about physical contact.* Reiki comes from the heart, not the hands. Although physical contact may be part of the Reiki practice, it is not the most important part. The most important part of session is the heart to heart connection that can happen.

- *Respect the herd.* Remember that when you are sharing Reiki with your horses, you are in their home. It is always best to consider yourself a humble guest. Always be open to all the horses in the area. Don't ignore the alpha horse in the pasture. Be sure to greet each horse that comes to you. In a herd situation, you should ask the alpha's permission to share Reiki. Sometimes the alpha will share Reiki first, but hopefully, if you've respected their leadership appropriately, he/she will walk away and allow you to connect with whatever horse you want to focus on. If not, you can always try again another time.

## *The Horse Session*

With the above ethics in mind, here's a guide to the best practices in sharing Reiki with your horses.

1. Place yourself somewhere near your horses. You can stay outside the fence if you like. If they are willing, you can greet them with physical contact and a quiet voice.

2. When you are ready to begin, simply set your intention that you are opening your heart to create a beautiful healing space of peacefulness for this horse if they would like to connect with you. This intention is very open and leaves the horse in charge, therefore it is a way of "asking permission."

3. If you did greet your horse with physical contact, take a few steps back so you are several feet away and begin your Reiki meditation. Rest your hands at your sides or on your lower belly. If your horse walks away, don't give up too soon—continue to focus on the meditation and see if he returns to you. Embrace your horse's movement and keep your focus inward. Only if a horse seems unhappy with your presence should you stop the session and leave the space.

4. Ideally, your state of mind should be peaceful and open, but it is natural to lose focus and for your mind to wander. When this happens, simply revisit the meditation to help you to refocus your energy.

5. Allow enough time for the horse to relax fully and connect with you; thirty to sixty minutes is ideal. Within this time frame, it is natural for your horse to come and go into and out of the connection. They will show this transition with physical movement closer to you or farther away, or by becoming extremely relaxed and then becoming more active, and so on.

Just as your mind may wander and come back, it is very typical for animals to share Reiki in an "ebb and flow" fashion, and the more flexible and comfortable you are with this movement/activity, the more successful you will be in connecting.

6. Pay attention to what your horse is telling you by his/her behavior. Mirror movements to show respect for your horse's feelings about the session. Rest your hands gently on the horse if he approaches you and shows interest in physical contact.

Signs of connection and relaxation (even something as simple as grazing nearby) show that your horse is enjoying the session.

7. At the end of the session, thank your horse for connecting with you. Set your intention to finish your meditation. Take a few moments to pet/talk to your horse if he/she is open to that.

## *Empowering Horse People*

If we get the opportunity to share Reiki with someone's horse, it is ideal to also share Reiki with the horse's person. Our health is closely tied to our horse by our close relationship, and chances are, if the horse needs healing, so does his person! In addition, sometimes the best way to explain to people what their horses might feel during a Reiki session is to let them experience Reiki for themselves. On the whole, I find that Reiki responses are better with horses if their people are included in the sessions, sometimes because the person is then in a better state of mind to support the horse, but also because sometimes horses feel more open to connecting when they see their people also being helped. Yes, they love us that much!

Physical touch during a Reiki session should only be used

with horses when they come forward and request it, however with humans, we are such tactile creatures, that physical touch is the standard protocol.

## *The Reiki Touch*

All Reiki touch is very gentle, however here are four levels of touch you can choose when offering Reiki. When sharing Reiki with a person, you can follow your intuition and you can also ask the person to let you know if they are not comfortable at any time.

1. Light touch: Hands are held flat against the body with light touch.
2. Lighter touch: Only the heel of the hand and the tips of the fingers touch the body.
3. Lightest touch: Only the tips of the fingers touch the body.
4. Aura touch: Hands are positioned just off the body.

The type of touch you use (or don't use) doesn't make Reiki more or less effective, except that we always want our clients to feel comfortable and supported. Remember, Reiki comes from the heart, not the hands.

## *Human/Horse Sessions*

There are two ways to bring a person into the Reiki session with the horse: offering a human chair session with the horse nearby, or sharing a standing session with the person and horse together.

## The Human Chair Session with the Horse

Sharing Reiki with people while they are sitting in a chair is a convenient way to share Reiki with humans wherever they may be: in a tack room, next to a paddock or in a barn. To bring the horse into the human's session, find a place near the horse, but safely outside the enclosure, and ask the person to sit in the chair. Have her set her intention that she is open to healing, close her eyes and relax. Set your intent to support the healing space for this person and also invite the horse to share in the space in whatever way is comfortable. Using Reiki touch, place your hands one-by-one on these five positions, holding each for approximately 3-5 minutes: the forehead, the sides of the head, the forehead/back of head, the shoulders, and the top of the head. You can also follow your intuition with timing and add any other positions to which you are drawn.

Mostly likely, after only a very short time, the person will become very relaxed and let go of all the stresses from the day. Stay aware of the response of the horse. Because horses are so sensitive, they are able to step into the peaceful space you create with the chair session. If the horse chooses to share the session, you will see signs of connection and relaxation from him.

## Standing Session with the Horse

For this type of session, stand with the horse's person near the horse and lead the person in one of the Reiki meditations in this book. Both you and the person can begin with hands on the lower belly to help create a grounded energy. After visualizing the meditation, stand quietly with eyes open and aware of the horse's movements. When you feel centered, you can slowly expand your hands out from your belly and invite the horse to share the space. If the horse comes forward, show the person how to place the hands lightly wherever the horse is offering. You may also place your hands on the person's shoulders, standing behind them to support the quiet, peaceful space created by the meditation. Or stand next to the person with one hand on their lower back and your other hand on the horse. Use your intuition, and keep your state of mind quiet and open, allowing yourself to respond naturally to any movement of the horse. You can help the person to mirror the movement of the horse, and return to your meditation if your mind wanders. Your intent is simply to support the connection of the horse and his person, without expectations. I love this type of session, as it is like watching a beautiful healing dance between two hearts.

## *How do we know Reiki is helping?*

Often people want to see something miraculous or amazing to show that sharing Reiki meditation with their horses is helping. And it's true that I have seen my share of amazing moments in Reiki. However, for me, the most important thing that shows me that Reiki is working is looking at my own life. Am I living more compassionately, with more of an open heart? Am I more mindful in my everyday life? These are the most important indications that Reiki is working. Do the horses respond? Are they feeling better? Yes, that will also be a result: peace and well-being for our equine friends, but it is my own personal experience that has really given me a deep trust in Reiki that is unshakeable.

I have had breast cancer twice, and I know from this very difficult experience that the practices of Reiki helped save my life. I also had the help of conventional medicine, such as surgery and radiation—but it was a very difficult mental/emotional journey (not to mention physical and spiritual!), and my meditation practice was my shining light through many dark days. Reiki helped me to find my way back to true wellness; I had to learn how to heal my mind, heart, and spirit so that I could continue on even stronger. Reiki did that for me. Reiki is amazing! And I know without a shadow of a doubt that it can do the same for our horses.

So that gives me a tremendous peace of mind when I am sharing Reiki with a horse. I also know that each being on this earth has his/her own unique journey. It isn't for me to say what that journey looks like, however, I have a very deep sense that Reiki always shifts things in transformational ways, even if it may sometimes be too subtle for us to see with our eyes.

Typical "yes" responses to Reiki from a horse include signs of relaxation such as lowering of the head, licking and chewing, yawning, a loose and hanging lip, and so on. If your horse is eating, he may simply relax and eat, occasionally giving you eye contact or putting his nose in your hand.

Typical "maybe" responses to Reiki include more tentative behaviors: Perhaps the horse will not completely relax, however, he will stay near you, or at least keep his focus on you during all or part of the session.

Typical "no" responses to Reiki include irritated or aggravated behavior. If the horse is clearly annoyed at your presence and wants you to leave, you know he is saying, "No, thanks—not today." In this case we must always respect the horse's wishes. Even if in our minds we think they "need" healing, and we want very badly for them to connect with us, it is not for us to decide this. We can always try again another time. I find that sometimes a horse who says no to Reiki is testing us to see if we are really going to listen and respect his decision. Often when we come back the next time they are much more receptive, because we have shown them that we are not pushing our own agenda. Horses really appreciate being given this kind of respect. When we remember that Reiki is about connecting from the heart, and the healing that flows naturally from that open-hearted space, we will be much more successful in gaining horses' trust and openness.

## Case Study: *Reiki for Opie*
## by Ann Asadorian

A friend from the barn asked me to share Reiki with her horse Opie, who had just had minor surgery on his leg. Opie is a big, off-the-track Thoroughbred with an attitude as big as his size. He loves his special person, but has little patience for anyone else! Needless to say, I stood close by outside of his stall and did not attempt physical contact as I began. As Opie stood at the back of his stall, eyeing me and wondering what this was all about, I quietly asked his permission to share Reiki with him. He nibbled on some hay as I settled into my meditation. Picturing bright, healing energy emanating from my entire body and surrounding him had a profound effect. I could sense his tense energy being replaced by calm. He quieted and came to the front of the stall to stand by me for a moment. Soon he became anxious and started to pace the stall. I thought this was a signal that he had had enough, but I remained in the moment because I felt a strong connection between us. Within minutes, Opie moved to the side of the stall, lowered his head, and drifted off to sleep. I stayed with him for several more minutes as he slept. As I turned to leave, I noticed that all of the horses in the barn were quietly resting in the tranquility that had been created by Reiki.

## Case Study: *Always Honor Choice*
## by Cathy O'Brien

One of my first experiences sharing Reiki with a horse was with Las Vegas Dancer, a former racehorse at the sanctuary Pregnant

Mare Rescue. Very pregnant, Las Vegas had a reputation as a difficult horse, a diva. I fell in love with her instantly. As I stood outside her stall offering Reiki, I felt a strong connection with her. She came closer to me against the edge of the stall, her back end toward me. I sensed that, like many pregnant women, her lower back hurt. I felt invited to do hands-on Reiki, so I placed my hands gently through the fence onto her lower back. We stood like that for a while, in a beautiful and loving meditative connection. After a while, she walked away and moved to the other side of her stall, very relaxed. When the session was over, before I left, she walked back over to me and gave me a little nuzzle on the lips and let me kiss her. I was thrilled! I loved the connection I felt with her and felt so grateful for the experience.

Then I went to do Reiki with another horse, Dually. Everyone had said that Dually loved connecting with Reiki, especially hands-on. Well, he didn't want it from me. He wanted nothing to do with me. I tried to get quiet and offer the connection, but if I got anywhere near him, he put his ears back and stepped away. I finally gave up. It could be that our energy didn't sync. It could be that he'd had enough Reiki for the day or just wasn't in the mood. I don't know.

What I learned is that either way, you can't take it personally. This is why we give animals the choice. Sometimes they want Reiki, sometimes they don't, and it's always up to them.

## **Case Study: *Moose Moves***
## **by Camille Pukay**

My first day at the River Bluff Rescue Ranch with the rescue horses was amazing. I first shared Reiki standing outside of Big Joe and Moose's stalls. Big Joe approached immediately to check out my hands and then stood at the back of his stall. Because of this reaction, I felt comfortable moving inside his stall, sharing Reiki from a short distance. Big Joe dozed for thirty minutes, then perked up, arched his head up and back for a huge stretch, and fell back to sleep.

I noticed Moose eyeing me curiously from his stall. So I chose to share Reiki with Moose by standing outside his stall. He immediately approached and stood near my hands; I felt intense heat from my left hand as he dozed for fifteen minutes. When he woke up, he became interested in something that was occurring down the hall, so I figured he was done and I left. Five minutes later, my sister told me Moose was looking for me. This time, I stepped into his stall to offer Reiki.

He immediately stood directly in front of me, so I placed my left hand between his eyes and my right hand on his throat. A few minutes later, he rocked slowly back and forth, sensing the energy from my hands. His facial expression was pure delight! Then he slowly walked past me, turned his head to look at me and backed straight into me with his behind in my face. I immediately jumped to the side, thinking, "What the heck?" but he turned and looked at me, repositioned himself, and slowly backed straight into me again! I jumped to the side again, thinking, "No way am I standing directly behind you!" and placed my hands on his rear end from the side. I quickly stepped out of his stall and shut the door. For the third time, Moose slowly backed himself directly in front of me with his tail sticking out. I placed my right hand on his tailbone and my left hand on his left hip.

Within minutes, Moose released a huge sigh and buckled his left rear leg in a relaxed pose as he lowered his head near the ground. We stood there for twenty minutes, and midway through I burst into huge tears! It was as if he were releasing his emotions through me. When he was finished, Moose slowly turned around and stood directly in front of me to thank me, while tears still fell down my face. I told Elizabeth, the ranch owner, what happened.

Her chin literally dropped and she said, "You touched his tail? And hip? Moose has never let anybody touch his tail or hip. They are extremely painful areas for him, and no one has been able to touch them voluntarily!"

This story has a happy ending. Eight months later, Moose was adopted to a wonderful forever home!

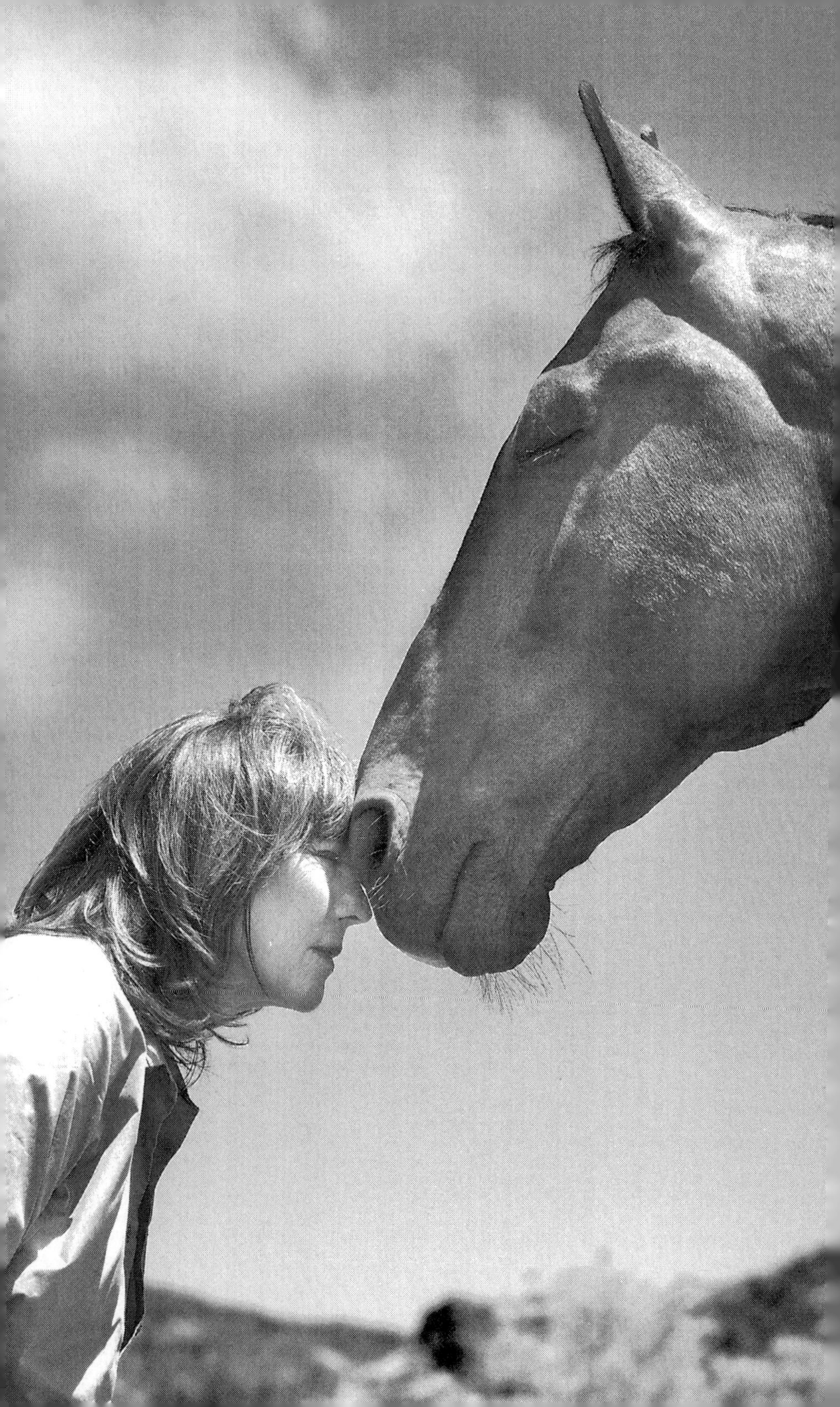

## CHAPTER 12
# Communication and Reiki

*"We have two ears and only one tongue in order that we may hear more and speak less."*

—Diogenes Laertius

PEOPLE OFTEN ASK me how animal communication relates to sharing Reiki with a horse, and if we need to receive "messages" from the horse to be able to help them. Equine Reiki and animal communication are related and yet separate.

Sharing Reiki actually *is* communication, in the sense that it's just a deeper level of connecting. It's more of a spiritual communion rather than a two-way communication with the animal; in its highest aspects, sharing Reiki is about merging with the essence of your horse. When you're meditating with your horse, you create a peaceful Reiki space where there's no separation: no you and no horse. Sharing Reiki is simply a beautiful communing of souls.

But what if people ask us to share Reiki with their horses and then want an answer to some kind of question? Many people assume that when we share Reiki, some kind of psychic information will come through. When I began this journey of sharing Reiki with animals, I was very conscious of and focused on what I was receiving during a session. I focused on how I could explain things to the horse's person, share the insights I had, and so on. But what I found over time was that often things shifted in spite of what I had discussed with the person. In other words, the healing journey seemed to have a mind of its own, above and beyond our human ruminations, hopes, wishes, and worries. So over time, I moved away from trying to interpret things for discussion with the horse's person, and instead focused on just being open.

For me, the real power of Reiki lies in my own personal, meditative spiritual practice. Reiki meditation draws us into a deeper space, one that is the most healing for ourselves and is also the place to which horses are most drawn when we are with them. It is a place without words and without judgments: that deep, quiet space where language has no meaning. My best advice about what to do when receiving intuitive information is to keep letting go: letting go of mind, of impressions, of judgments and of interpretations.

> *"You should therefore cease from practice based on intellectual understanding, pursuing words and following after speech, and learn the backward step that turns your light inwardly to illuminate your self."*
>
> —Dogen

This quote hints at the power of dropping the mind into the heart by turning inward rather than focusing our attention outward. In contrast to Reiki itself, communication with a horse often deals with the layers of the horse's being that are outside of the spiritual layer: the mental, emotional, and physical layers that are more connected with this lifetime's journey. In order to be successful at communication, we have to practice focusing on what we can pick up and then interpret and express it to the horse's people. So communication works with a layer just below the surface. Sometimes it can also dip into the spiritual, however, communication limits our ability to go deeply into this layer because it requires a dualistic frame of reference in order to interpret and express through language. In other words, communication requires a two-way framework—therefore there are two beings involved. Sharing Reiki focuses on merging the two beings into One.

What I find more profound than trying to interpret a horse's message for a person is going even deeper, resisting the allure of language, judgment, and interpretation, and simply holding a meditative space of peace and healing for the horse—and I prefer to also include the family of the horse (both human and non-human) in that practice. Reiki can create a space of wisdom and clarity for all so that when they are ready, and at the perfect moment, they can realize all that they need to know, and knowing it for themselves from a very deep place. When wisdom comes to us in this kind of way, internally and authentically, at the right moment, then it really sticks and creates a profound shift in our inner being.

If I'm going to talk about the Reiki session, I prefer to talk more about the heart connection I felt. Perhaps the feeling was very peaceful. Or I might talk about the horse's behavior during the session, for example, if he fell asleep or maybe pushed a shoulder or hip into my hands. I simply leave it at that, without an added layer of my own interpretation. I will also ask the person to watch for any kind of healing shift, either in the area that they had hoped for and expected, or in another area of their horse's health, because that's also significant. This is because the origins of our health conditions are often unknown, and what we see with our eyes is only the most outer layer of the issue.

For example, a horse with a skin condition who receives Reiki might show a post-Reiki shift in emotional behavior. The two are related—perhaps the physical issue is caused by an emotional imbalance—yet this might not be easily seen at first.

Rather than the horse's person looking to me for advice, I prefer that each person work to put together his own understanding. I think the awareness of healing is more powerful when it comes from the person's own light bulb moment, rather than from something an outsider says. In addition, it's very important to remember that any kind of diagnosis or health information should always come from a veterinarian. I've seen a few situations where animal communicators shared information that was in conflict with the vet's program, which caused a lot of upset and worry for the horse, the person, and the vet. I can't emphasize enough how important it is that holistic practitioners always follow the lead of the supervising veterinarian.

Sharing Reiki actually takes a lot of pressure off us as practitioners, because with Reiki, we don't manipulate energy, we don't diagnose or cure conditions, and we don't actually "do" the healing. Reiki supports the horse to heal himself. Reiki creates a space that can transcend the limits and boundaries of language, even melt away the differences between species, and in this open space, miracles of healing can happen! In sharing Reiki, we can simply *be* with the person and their horse. With our open heart and compassionate presence, we can see attitudes, situations, and emotions all shift towards balance, understanding, and acceptance.

Sharing Reiki can bring compassionate presence to the ups and downs of any healing situation. We can become supportive listeners and witnesses, always remaining peaceful and grounded. Even through the hard parts, when people are in denial or get angry and frustrated, our Reiki practice helps us to just hold the space—gently, openly, and without judgment. To be able to sit in a grounded, peaceful space through all of that heavy emotion—

without getting knocked over by it—is a beautiful gift we can offer to horses, their people, and to ourselves. This is how sharing Reiki can bring about transformational healing, love, and acceptance.

When we share Reiki, we also nurture the empowerment of the horse and his people. In the peaceful, meditative space which is beyond language and interpretation, where there is no conversation or discussion—in that deeper place resides true compassion, as well as the capacity to access our own deepest wisdom and true miracles of healing potential. That's the place I want to nurture through Reiki, both in myself and in the people and horses I work with. I want to dig deep into my meditation and then just let go into that quiet space. How do we dig so deep? There is no shortcut; we just have to practice meditation every day.

Some of you reading this might be more drawn to the communication aspect of connecting with horses, and you might see Reiki meditation as simply a support for your communication. I have heard many of my students tell me that meditating with Reiki techniques really enhanced and strengthened their communication skills, and I think that's great. As you can tell from this chapter, I'm kind of a Reiki purist, but it's good to follow your own heart in this.

## *Luke, master of communication*

My trainer's horse Luke is a master of communicating his needs during Reiki sessions, so much so that my trainer decided to learn Reiki, and one day when Luke was very uncomfortable, she decided to share Reiki with him. That particular day, she had used all her horse knowledge, but still couldn't isolate the problem area. We decided to share Reiki with Luke together. I guided her through a meditation, reminding her simply to connect with her heart and allow her horse to lead. It was a beautiful thing to watch the connection between Luke and Susan within the Reiki session. Within a few minutes, Luke lifted his head and looked at her, clearly asking for her to come closer. As she placed her hands on his shoulder, the most incredible thing took place: Luke began to shake his skin over and over, literally moving Susan's hands upward and backward across his back, toward his hind end. After a few moments, he stopped his skin movement, settling into deep relaxation. She felt heat and pain in her hands from this area of his body.

She realized he had guided her to his problem spot! The next day she shared with me that not only had his problem improved tremendously, but also that their connection with each other seemed to have deepened: It was as if they could now communicate with each other even more effortlessly than before. She also joked that she was comforted by the fact that even if she was pretty clueless, her horse was happy to step in and show her what to do.

## Case Study: *Connecting to Horses*
## by Ariel Dove

Just the other day I shared Reiki with a horse that has issues with anxiety. His person often has to spend a long time each day working through this anxiety when she is riding; sometimes she can't work through it at all. This particular day, the horse was turned out in a large field. I came into the field but stayed at a bit of a distance, not approaching him. He came up to me, pushed his nose into my hands as if to say, "Yes, please," and then walked twenty feet away to lie down for the duration of the session. He sighed, yawned, rolled completely on his side and fell asleep. It was quite incredible to see him just let go and completely relax!

When he had enough, he simply got up, walked over to me, and pushed his nose into my chest for a hug. It was a real "thank you" moment. Several hours later, his person rode him. She was so excited and amazed, she called me immediately afterward, saying, "Can you always Reiki my horse before I ride?" Apparently, he had been completely relaxed and responsive during the entire ride, with no anxiety at all! I knew that allowing him to move back and forth freely in his pasture while we were connecting was key in helping him to be able to trust, relax, let go, and heal.

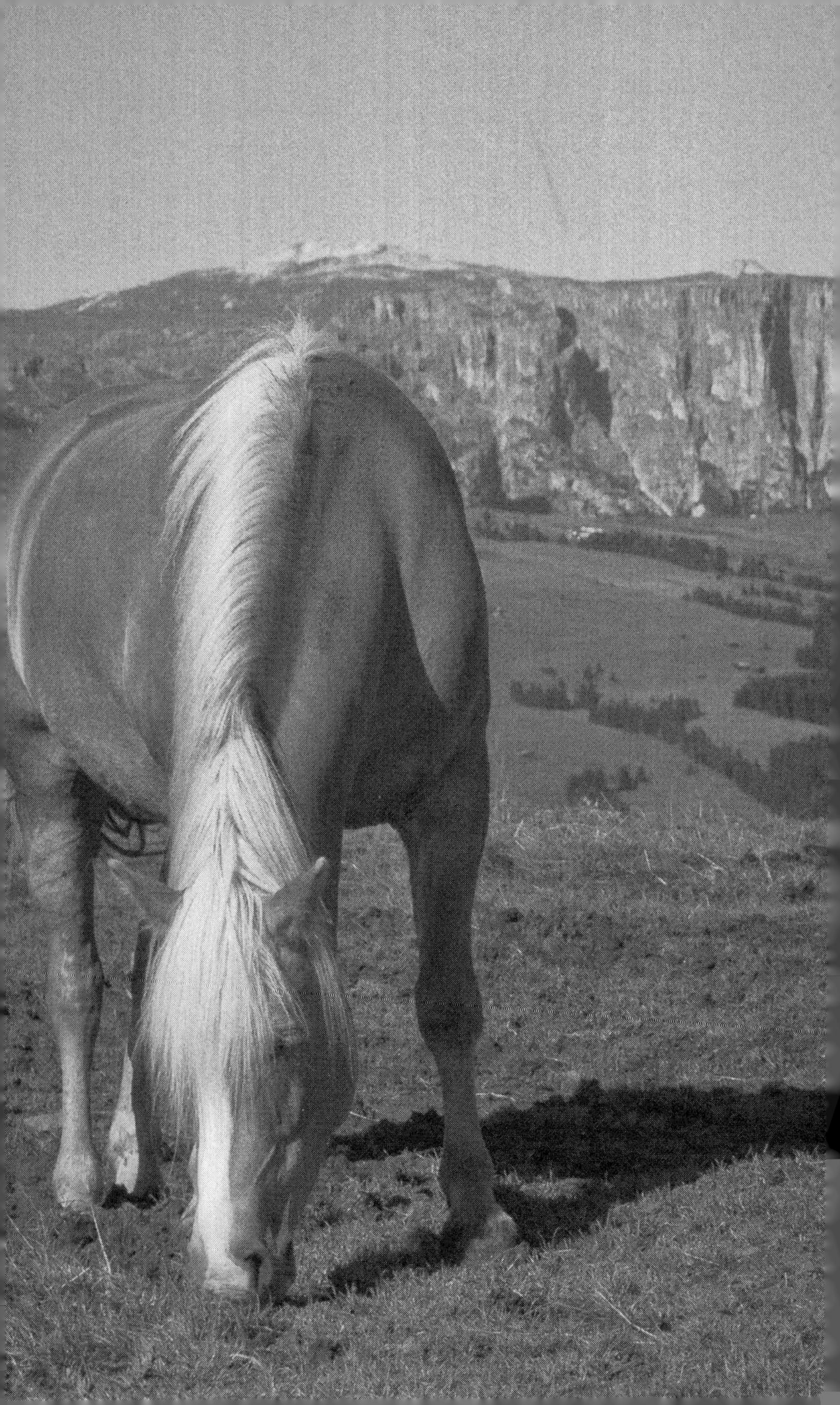

# Earth and Sky Meditation with Your Horse

***Tip:*** *Practice this exercise while standing several feet from your horse, arms at your sides, eyes open with a soft gaze downward about three feet in front of you. Allow your horse to move freely as he or she wishes. Allow thirty to sixty minutes to practice.*

Take a deep breath. Let it out slowly. Take another deep breath. Let it out slowly. Imagine that all of the stresses from your day can be released from you with each exhale. Breathe in. Exhale slowly. Allow yourself to let go of all your concerns and just be aware of your breath.

Imagine there are roots coming down from the base of your spine. These roots stretch far down into the earth, grounding you. Feel yourself stable, grounded, and part of the earth, just as if you were a beautiful tree. Imagine that the grounding energy of the earth can flow up your roots into your heart center, giving you stability and peace. For several minutes, breathe deeply as earth energy flows within your being. Feel peace and calm coming upward from the earth and flowing within your whole body, each breath anchoring you more strongly and deeply into the earth's power and stability.

Now imagine that the expansive, creative energy of the sky is flowing down into the top of your head. It is a beautiful shower of light and healing, which brings with it spiritual and intuitive wisdom, and all things good and positive. It flows from your head into your heart. Bringing this bright energy into your heart allows it to open and expand. Within your heart is all the highest love, compassion, and harmony that exists in the universe. Feel earth and sky energies mingling in your heart center, your heart getting brighter and brighter. Imagine earth energy coming up and sky energy coming down, mixing together and flowing out until you feel the beautiful light that is shining at your heart begin to expand to encompass your whole being.

Feel your heart shining brighter with each inhale, and expanding wider and wider all around you with each exhale. Feel your heart expanding out your skin into your aura, into the area around you, and infinitely out into the universe. Feel that with each breath you can also expand love, compassion, and harmony outward, creating a space that your horse can step into if he or she wishes.

As you stand in this peaceful, beautiful light that you have created with your mind and breath, simply invite your horse into the space. You can do so directly with your voice, silently in your mind, or by setting a quiet intention to share your heart. Simply stand with your horse in this peaceful space and *be* with him.

After your horse has relaxed for a period of time, he may wake up, walk away, or show interest in other things. This is an indication that the session is over. Take a moment to thank him for connecting with you in this beautiful space, set your intention to finish and take a nice deep cleansing breath.

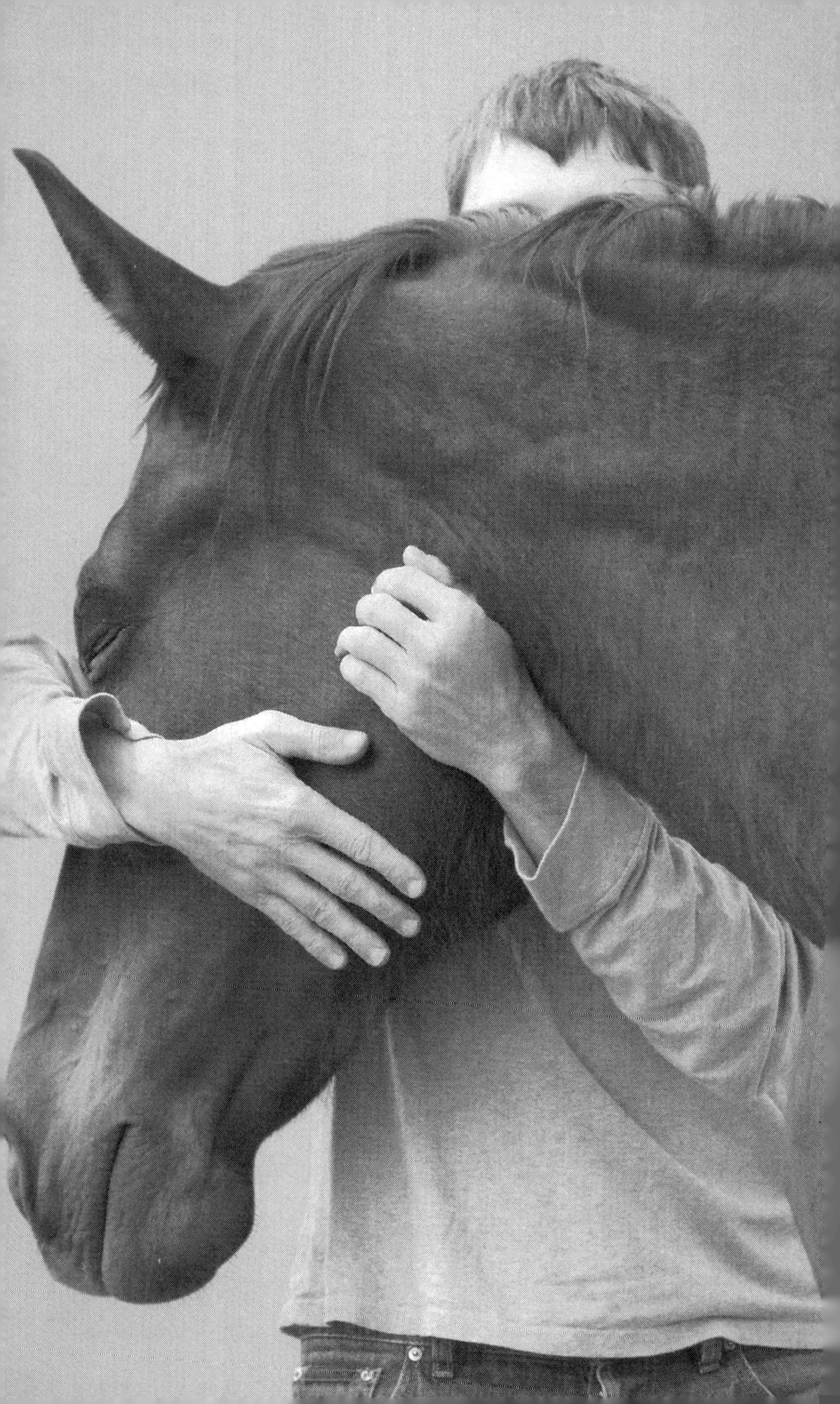

# CHAPTER 13
# Saying Goodbye

*A compassionate person is the most powerful healer, not only of their own disease and other problems, but of those of others. A person with loving kindness and compassion heals others simply by existing.*

—Lama Zopa Rinpoche

I LOVE THIS QUOTE because for me it represents the real truth about what it means to be a Reiki practitioner. Reiki is about the healing power of *being*. This is most evident when supporting horses through the dying process, because since there is nothing more we can *do*, we are forced to truly *be*.

I will always remember the first time a horse I knew passed away. This was a very old horse who lived at a barn where I kept my horse years ago. He had been having problems standing and walking for quite some time. I was aware of what was going on with him, often taking time to pet him and talk to him. He was very sweet. One day, I was getting my horse's grain and I felt someone was watching me. I looked up and there was this old horse, staring straight at me. He had somehow wandered away from his usual little area, as he had free run of the ranch.

He was standing about twenty feet from me. He had come toward me, and he was facing me directly and was looking intently at me. At first I thought he was looking for grain, but his ears were pricked and he was looking so hard at me. I suddenly realized he wanted something deeper. Somehow he sensed that I was someone whom he could trust to be truly present with him at this difficult time. I walked towards him just a couple of feet, so that I was maybe fifteen feet away. I knelt down on the ground and told him, "I am here for you right now." I just opened my heart with love. Immediately he knelt and lay down. He then gave a big sigh and put his head down on the ground.

I could feel that he was just so tired, and so ready to go out of this existence. I began to meditate to help me stay grounded; meanwhile, a crowd was starting to gather. When I was growing up, my dad called this type of crowd the "Uh-Oh Squad," as in, "Uh-oh! The old horse has gone down. Uh-oh! What should we do? Uh-oh! He's not even lifting his head!" Amid the panic of the crowd, I knew my Reiki meditation could help me to remain peaceful and open-hearted, creating a calming space for this horse.

I was able to connect with him for a little while longer, until his people arrived and the vet came. He passed away later that night. When I went into the barn the next day, he was gone—and yet I could still clearly feel his presence. I kept seeing him out of the corner of my eye—then I would turn my head, and he would not be there.

He had lived his whole life at this ranch. He had been born there and died in his late twenties. I felt his spiritual presence there strongly; it was really beautiful. What a gift that I was able to sense him in this spiritual way. What a gift to be able to connect with another being even after his physical body has passed!

This is a special gift of working with Reiki meditation: it can help us to understand that our physical life is not all there is, because our energy or spirit, which is really our true essence, continues on.

This experience opened my eyes to the possibilities of how Reiki could support more animals in my life than I had realized, and of course later on I discovered BrightHaven Animal Hospice, which is where I have taught so many Reiki classes. I've worked with many animals who were in their final days at BrightHaven, but this special old horse was one of my very first teachers about death and Reiki. Or, I should say, he was my teacher about the cycle of life; he taught me that death is not the end. He was such a gift because it was such a gentle experience, and so it was an easy introduction for me to this process. I will always be very grateful to him for that.

The Reiki precepts point to ways for us to support the dying process. Because horses are so sensitive to our moods and feelings, they will sense our distress and grief as they approach the time of transition. This can cause them concern and worry for us. By using healing meditations and the Reiki precepts, we can help ourselves to stay in a more balanced emotional state, which in turn helps our horses relax so that they can focus on their own inner journey of transition. Becoming a partner and helper to our horse as he or she passes will be one of the hardest things we will do in this life, but how could we do any less? Our love and gratitude for all the joy they have brought to our lives will carry us through.

*Just for today, do not anger.* We might feel anger at not being able to "cure" our horse, that we couldn't stop the progression of an illness, or anger at ourselves that we didn't notice it earlier, take different actions, or otherwise find ourselves able to stop things from progressing to this point. We must learn to surrender to what *is*, rather than obsess about what might have been. It is always easy to look back and second-guess oneself, but spending emotional energy on anger will only take away from the energy you have to support your horse's journey.

*Just for today, do not worry.* We might worry about what this transition will look like, if our horse will be in pain, and what each day might hold for our loved one. Our fear of the unknown can be very intimidating. Facing this uncertainty and surrendering to it will help us to remain present and courageous as we navigate the unknown, together with our horses.

*Be humble.* We might wish we could control the journey, making it smooth and easy for everyone concerned. We must learn to accept the dying process, whatever it might look like, in all its complexity and mysteriousness. Dying is a spiritual experience beyond our comprehension, a part of the cycle of life that we all must experience at some point. Being able to be there as a simple and humble witness to the process will provide much comfort for our horses.

*Be honest.* Our relationships with our horses always come from the deepest, most honest places within ourselves—after all, they will accept nothing less from us. In turn, our openness and honesty at this particular time in our horses' lives, as they approach death, is the most precious gift we can offer. The most healing we can offer is to be mindful and open-hearted, whatever the journey may look like. Reiki practice reminds us to be open and honest about all that this present moment contains: all the joy and sorrow, all the fullness of our memories, all of our love and all of our gratitude for our relationship. While holding all of this with an open heart, we must allow our horse to take this journey in his own way, and we must strive to accept all that this entails as best as we can.

*Be compassionate.* When we must face our beloved horse's death, it is easy to be hard on ourselves, wanting to have been able to "fix" things. Often we might ask ourselves, "What more could I have done?" or "What could I have done differently?" Our horses love and accept us for whatever decisions we make, knowing that we loved them and did our best for them. Just as they always loved us unconditionally and completely throughout their lives, so, too, do they love us as we support them through the transition process. Just as we practice compassion for our horses, we must remember to be compassionate to ourselves as well. With Reiki, we can practice meditating every day to let go of regrets and guilt once they have passed.

Separation is only a perception, but the inner truth, the truth of the soul, is that we are all One. Reiki meditation can help us remember this, and this is such a comfort when we have lost a loved one.

Being able to remain grounded is the most helpful tool for supporting the transition process. Grounding is also one of Reiki's central teachings. Recently, my trainer Susan's horse Peru became unexpectedly ill. I had known Peru for several years, and as he was the bonded pasture buddy of my own horse Shawnee, I held a special place for him in my heart. One morning when we arrived at the barn, Peru was very ill and having trouble breathing. We would later learn that he had congestive heart failure, however, being such a stoic horse, we had no idea anything was wrong before this. Although he had had a cough for about a week, he had been doing well, schooling Prix St. Georges, a high level of dressage training. Now suddenly he was deathly ill.

By coincidence a local vet was visiting the farm that morning, and when she arrived, we could tell by the look on her face that this was extremely serious. She had to stabilize Peru before he could be taken to a nearby vet hospital.

The process of getting him ready to go took about three hours. During this time, I stood with Peru, my hands on his side, and imagined I was a mountain. The winds of emotion were blowing everywhere, but I stood strong and calm for him, for Susan, for the vet, and also for my dear Shawnee, who stood at a respectful distance and watched, nickering at me when I turned to look at him from time to time. Using my Reiki eyes, I managed to see Peru as his perfect beautiful light and spirit, even as his physical body was struggling so terribly. Peru managed to stay calm despite his difficulties in breathing, which I feel was such a credit to the power of Reiki.

As Susan drove him away to the hospital, Peru called to Shawnee, and Shawnee called back to Peru, and at that moment, I allowed myself to collapse into tears. I felt deep in my heart that this was their final goodbye, these two bonded friends.

At the hospital, Susan was given the diagnosis, and informed that there was nothing that could be done. Susan, her husband, her son, and a working student all entered his stall to say goodbye. Peru faced each of them in turn, gently resting his head against the front of each person's body. After staying with one for a bit, he moved on to the next, and so on, until he had said goodbye to each of them, in his own way.

The vet suggested to Susan that she not be there for the death, as it could be very unpleasant, however she insisted on being by his side. She stood with him and held him, and he passed completely peacefully, to the surprise of the attending medical personnel. The next day, when I spoke to Susan about the experience, she said, "Well, I was in no shape to do Reiki, but I was there for him with all my heart for every moment." I said to her, "You know, you just exactly described Reiki. That *is* Reiki."

Sometimes we think we have to be perfect meditators and healers, or at least almost as good as the Dalai Lama, to be able to create a healing space for someone we care for. The truth is that each of us has a heart and spirit that is powerful and bright, even when we are suffering, or facing difficulties. Love is the strongest force in the universe, and each of us has this infinite power of good and healing within us—we just have to remember it. Luckily for us, our animals bring it out in us! Sometimes we think Reiki is something separate from ourselves, something we somehow learn to "do." In reality, when we are mindfully present with another being, with a loving heart and compassionate mind—even in the face of death—that is when we have become whole. That is the perfect healing of *being* rather than *doing*; that is the power and essence of Reiki.

## Case Study: *Tenacious, My Priceless Teacher*
### by Tutie Brennan

It was not easy at first, realizing Tenacious's time to transition was coming soon. Having had him for over twenty years, just the thought of what life would be without him was impossible to imagine.

At age thirty-four, Tenacious, as his name implies, still hung on to life with vigor, joy, presence, and attitude. He thought well of himself as an aged stallion, and demonstrated his dignity and pride in being young at heart; alive and alert, he made it his business to know everything that was going on around him. As the time came for him to wind down, I noted that in those last few weeks he had little or no appetite. Yet he did not seem to mind.

Patiently, he waited, the spark still in his eye—it was not time yet. I would sit and share Reiki with him often. In the barn or in the paddock, he enjoyed dozing and relaxing as we shared Reiki meditation together. It was so peaceful to be in meditation with him; it was so blissful to be in the moment with him. It seemed with each Reiki session there grew an even deeper sense of both of our true natures. Those hours we shared are some of my most precious memories.

When at last the day did come, I felt we were both better prepared to accept the last step we would go through together in this lifetime. I sat up with Tenacious through the night, just the two of us. My Reiki practice helped me to look deeper; I no longer saw him as his physical body, but as his inner bright light. Whatever his physical body was doing did not matter much now. What was real was his Light. With Reiki, I was able to see beyond, and I was able to travel with him through his transition. This was an experience that is golden to me. After his spirit left the body, I felt such a calm and peace, wrapped in Love. Tenacious is still with me. I only have to let go, to be Reiki, be in the moment, and I can feel his essence. He is here.

Now a greater awareness has grown in me; I can see and feel a bit of Tenacious's Spirit in all horses. In a glimpse of an eye, there might be a familiar reflection, in a behavior, suddenly a spark I know, in a nuzzle and warm breath, a resonance I feel, and I will smile. I feel his energy. Sometimes I can even feel him as if his physical form is right by me! He is not gone, he is everywhere; and I know in Spirit we are all One. I give thanks for Reiki, where in Love and Compassion all things are possible. And I give thanks to a priceless Reiki teacher, Tenacious.

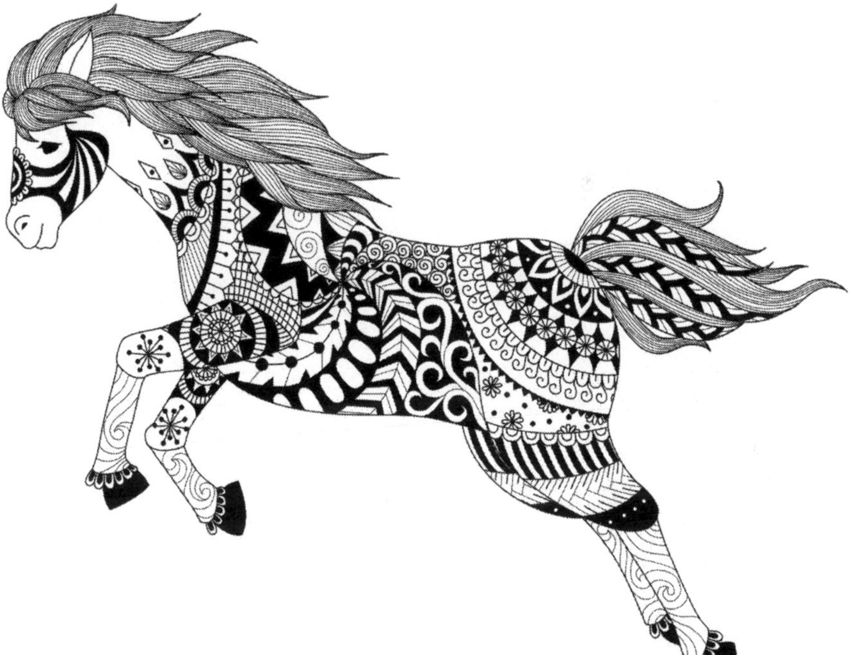

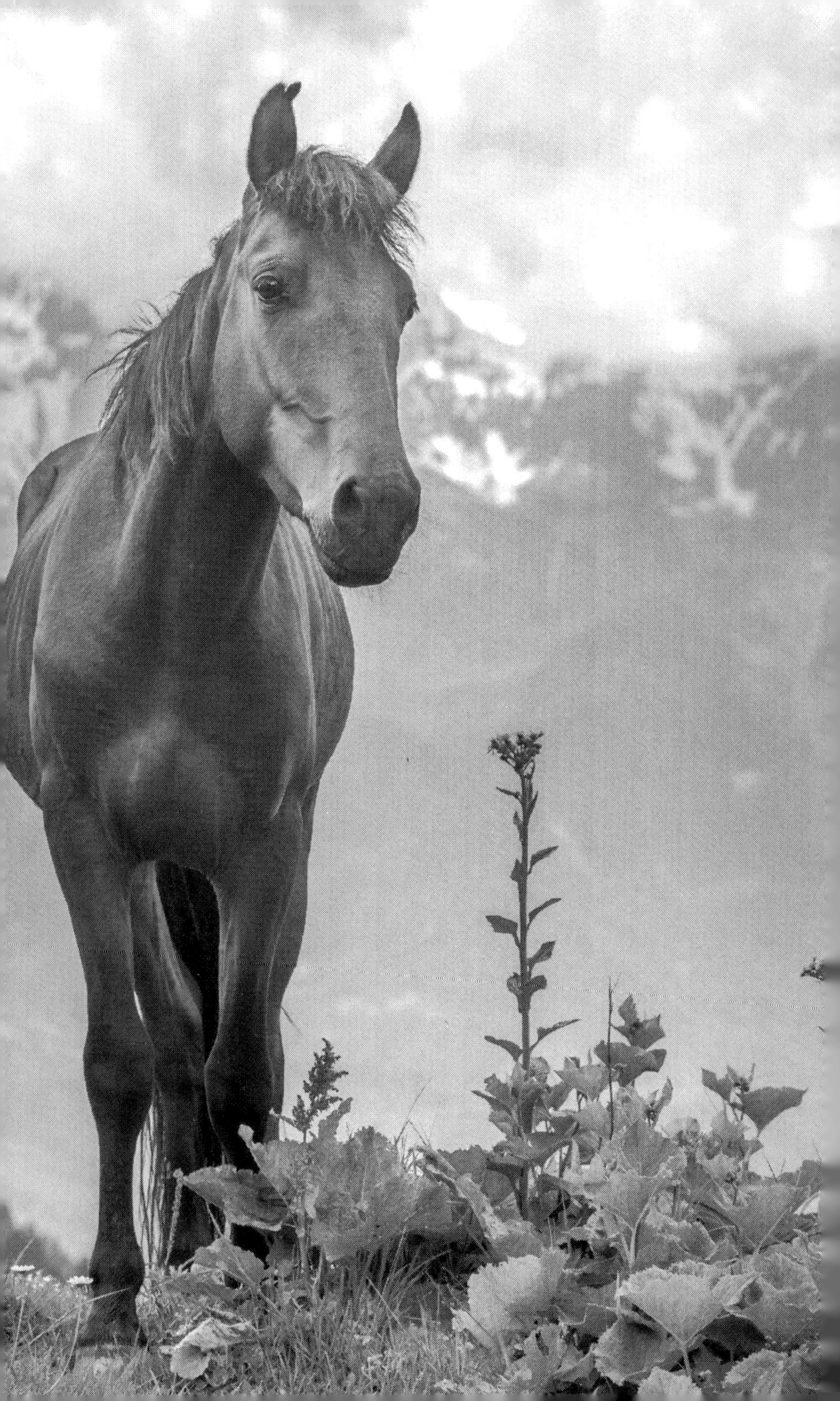

# Be the Mountain for Your Horse Meditation

Stand in the pasture/paddock with your horse. Place your hands over your lower belly and focus on the energy center below your navel, your *hara*. As you inhale, feel the breath as light flowing up from the earth into your legs and body and into your belly. On the exhale, feel the breath flowing from your lower belly down your legs and feet and returning to the earth. Imagine this light can travel instantaneously from your *hara* to the core of the earth and back again. With each breath, imagine the light grows brighter and brighter, both at your *hara* and in the core of the earth, the energy circulating back and forth. Feel your lower body becoming heavier and heavier, as if there is no separation between you and the earth's center.

After several minutes focusing on your breath, relax and just stand in the energy. Feel the energy in your *hara* as bright, warm light. Just as your hands are connected to the *hara*, all of your being is connected to your *hara*. Feel as if your *hara* is no different from the core of the earth. The same beautiful light emanates from your core and the earth's core. Feel the stability and strength of the earth within your own center.

Imagine this light can expand, filling your whole body with a beautiful bright light. Your inner light is the light of the earth—feel every cell of your body radiating the stability of earth. You are a mountain, even more, you are *all* mountains, and in fact you are the very planet.

Bring your awareness to the present moment. Feel the strength of earth ripple out your body into your emotions and into your spirit, making you stronger and stronger, just as the energy of earth ripples out into space. The earth moves in space, yet is stable and balanced within the universe. Your life changes unexpectedly, yet you are stable like a mountain; you are as balanced and strong as the earth itself.

Invite your horse to share this stable space with you. Don't try to *do* anything, or push the energy towards your horse. Just imagine that you *are* the mountain, you *are* the earth, and you are there, strong and stable, for your horse in this present moment. You are there for whatever this moment looks like, for whatever they might need. Share the space of strength, balance, and harmony for as long as you like. When you are ready to finish, thank your horse for his connection in this space, and take a nice deep breath as you slowly come back.

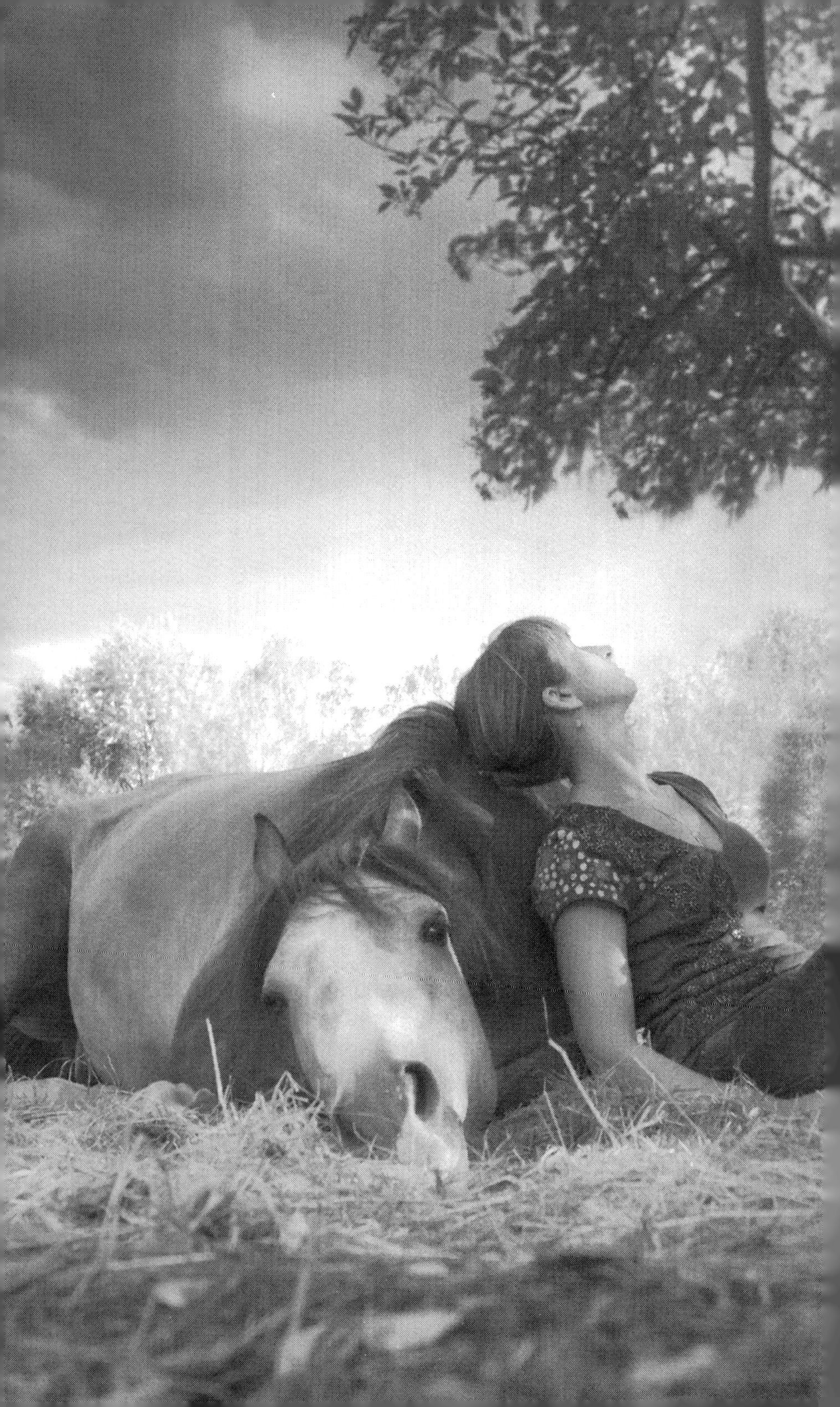

## CHAPTER 14
# How to Radiate Reiki

*"Your eyes will always be closer to your soul than any other part of your body, except the heart."*

—Sorin Cerin

MIKAO USUI, THE founder of the system of Reiki, was a master of many Japanese spiritual practices, and we can see this in the similarity Reiki teachings have to some Buddhist teachings. What I find amazing is that our horses, in their own ways, can teach us this same spiritual wisdom! One of the deepest ways to heal with your horse is to let go of separateness. What this really means is uncovering our true heart. It is our true heart that understands the truth of Oneness, that we are all connected in this beautiful, amazing universe.

Our human culture and society often cultivates separateness. Separation is only a perception, but the inner truth, the truth of the soul, is that we are all One. I often say that in order to realize this we need to learn to see with our Reiki eyes. Our hearts see to the truth of things. Our hearts see with wisdom and clarity. The practices of Reiki show us in many different ways how to open our hearts.

> "It is only with the heart that one can see rightly. What is essential is invisible to the eye."
>
> —Antoine de Saint-Exupéry

We humans put so much emphasis on what our eyes can see. The deeper lesson of Reiki meditation is letting go of our physical eyes, for then we can really *see*. When we truly *see*, compassion and healing will easily flow in abundance. Before we can overflow with compassion, we have to access our inner wisdom. Then the compassion, and the healing that follows, will pour out even without any effort on our part. This is why I have emphasized in this book meditation, turning inward and *being* quiet and peaceful, rather than focusing on chakras, hand positions and actions of *doing*.

We can see the relationship between healing and wisdom/compassion in the Buddhist symbol of the circle and the crescent. We often see this symbol, for example at the top of the Om symbol. We also see it in some other Buddhist symbols. In Buddhism, the moon represents compassion. The sun represents wisdom. Reiki practice helps us shine with the wisdom of our true self; in this way our lives will automatically reflect this through compassionate healing, just the way the sun shines and the moon reflects its beauty.

In Buddhism, Oneness is the union of wisdom and compassion. The sun really is the representation of the wisdom of emptiness, the idea that everything and nothing exists in the space of Oneness; the crescent moon symbolizes the development of Bodhichitta, which is our aspiration to awaken to this wisdom. So joining the sun and moon represents our inner wisdom awakening, and then our spontaneous compassion for all beings can just organically happen.

This brings us back to the Reiki precept of being compassionate to yourself and others. This precept is intertwined with wisdom; we can't really be compassionate without first realizing that we're all connected. Therefore, the more that we dissolve our feelings of separateness, the more compassion we can radiate in our lives. In turn, the more compassion we practice, the more happiness and wellness we have in our lives.

Throughout this book I have emphasized that practicing Reiki meditation teaches us that if we want to help our horses, it's really about finding balance within ourselves first. True healing is something that arises from within, from our deepest center of our being. It's not dependent upon outer circumstances or upon looking with our eyes. It's about seeing with our hearts, and that inner space of compassion creates an inner happiness, which is very stable, and very beautiful. It radiates out to the horses we love.

*"If you want others to be happy, practice compassion. If you want to be happy, practice compassion."*

—Dalai Lama

Horses have a beautiful way of opening our hearts. There's something about them and their presence in our lives that touches us the way nothing else does. When we sit in meditation with our horses, we feel that heart connection with them, compassion naturally arises and we and our horses feel happy. This happiness is the ultimate outcome of meditating with our horses.

Our horses already know about wisdom, compassion and joy. They hold a spiritual space of presence and openness that is a model for how we need to be living: purely, presently, without judgment, compassionate and open in our hearts. Practicing Reiki with our horses will create a beautiful space of compassion and great happiness inside of us. That inner happiness helps us to experience what true wellness and balance is all about. It helps us understand what it means to be healed; healing is so much bigger than the physical body. Compassion and joy heal in ways that nothing else can. Compassion and joy are also wonderful gifts our horses bring to our lives.

Horses also help us to see through to the heart of things. As humans, we might get stuck on the outer appearance or very often we get stuck in our intellectual mind, our reasoning mind, saying, "Oh, this is possible; that isn't possible." If we look at something with our intellectual mind, all we see are bits and pieces and separateness. But if we sit quietly with our horses, with an open heart, they will come forward to touch our hearts and show us that we are all connected. We are all One.

Practicing Reiki with our horses also helps us improve our ability to meditate, by quieting our minds. Our horses are great meditation partners. Their *way* and *being* are much quieter mentally and intellectually than ours. Their connection to wisdom is much deeper. When we share their energy within a meditative space, it can help shift us so that we become more open.

Remember to relax, trust and follow your horses' lead. Just think about how they always show us unconditional love no matter what, how they're always patient with us: even when we fail, even when we fall short, even when we don't do our best, even when we don't live up to our own expectations, even when we're not compassionate with ourselves, even when we're in the space of anger, even when we're in a space of worry, even when we're in a space of ego.

Remember, heart to heart healing goes both ways. Sometimes it is the most unlikely horses that teach us compassion. It might be the horse in the sanctuary who is very sick, or has been abused, and seems very weak. When we sit with this kind of horse in meditation, she will heal us. She will show us something about the heart and about what healing means. Observe yourself as you go into a situation to "help" this kind of horse—when you leave you may realize you received so much more than you offered.

Equine Reiki can open our hearts to miracles, open our hearts to a potential beyond what our intellectual minds are ready to accept. Our horses are already operating at a level of compassion and Oneness that we could only hope one day to somehow touch, even for a moment. We are so lucky because our horses are living here with us. They are here to be our spiritual teachers, if we only open our hearts to connect. We can do that through Reiki meditations that encourage us to spend time mindfully with the horses in our lives. In this way, we learn how to truly radiate Reiki.

## Case Study: *Angel*
## by Leah D'Ambrosio

Kathleen's nonprofit, the Shelter Animal Reiki Association, shares and teaches Reiki in many organizations all over the world. Pregnant Mare Rescue (PMR) is one of the horse rescue organizations that is open to Reiki. This particular day, I went to share Reiki with Angel at PMR. Angel was a mare rescued from slaughter by PMR with her new foal. Unfortunately, she had tripped and fallen at the sanctuary, and was extremely head-shy; for a whole week, the founder of PMR had tried without success to take her halter off. SARA practitioner Kim Slowick and I visited PMR one day and went out into the field to share Reiki with Angel. One of the main teachings of SARA is that animals must always lead the way with sessions, so we weren't sure if Angel would even accept Reiki.

Angel's response was amazing: within five minutes, she approached Kim and stood nearby, lowered her head, and sighed. Kim reached out to her, and Angel smelled her hand and relaxed further. Kim and I continued to share Reiki with Angel for about forty minutes. At the end of the treatment, the founder came into the pasture, gently approached Angel, and was able to easily and immediately slide the halter off Angel's head! We knew allowing Angel to lead her own Reiki session made all the difference in her trust. What an honor to share the Reiki space with Angel and witness her acceptance and transformation.

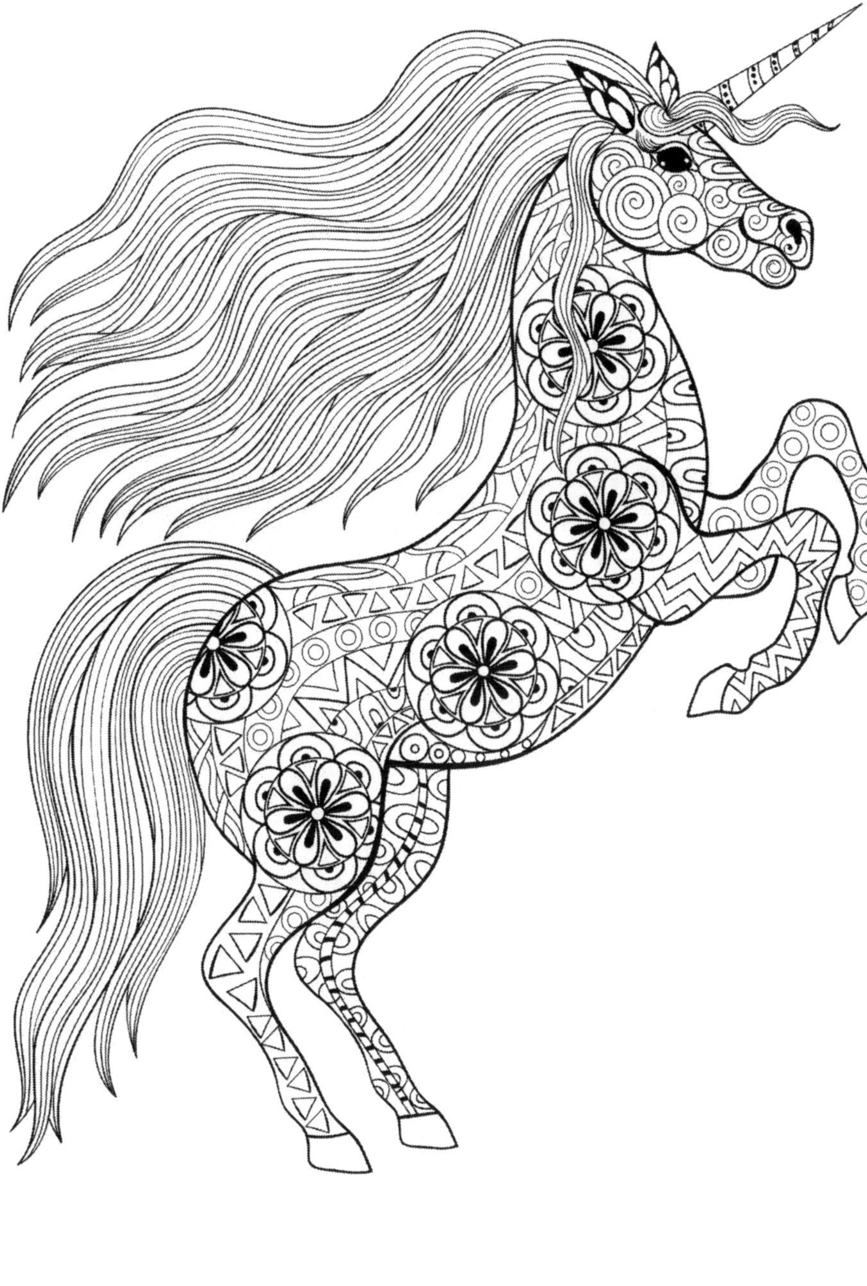

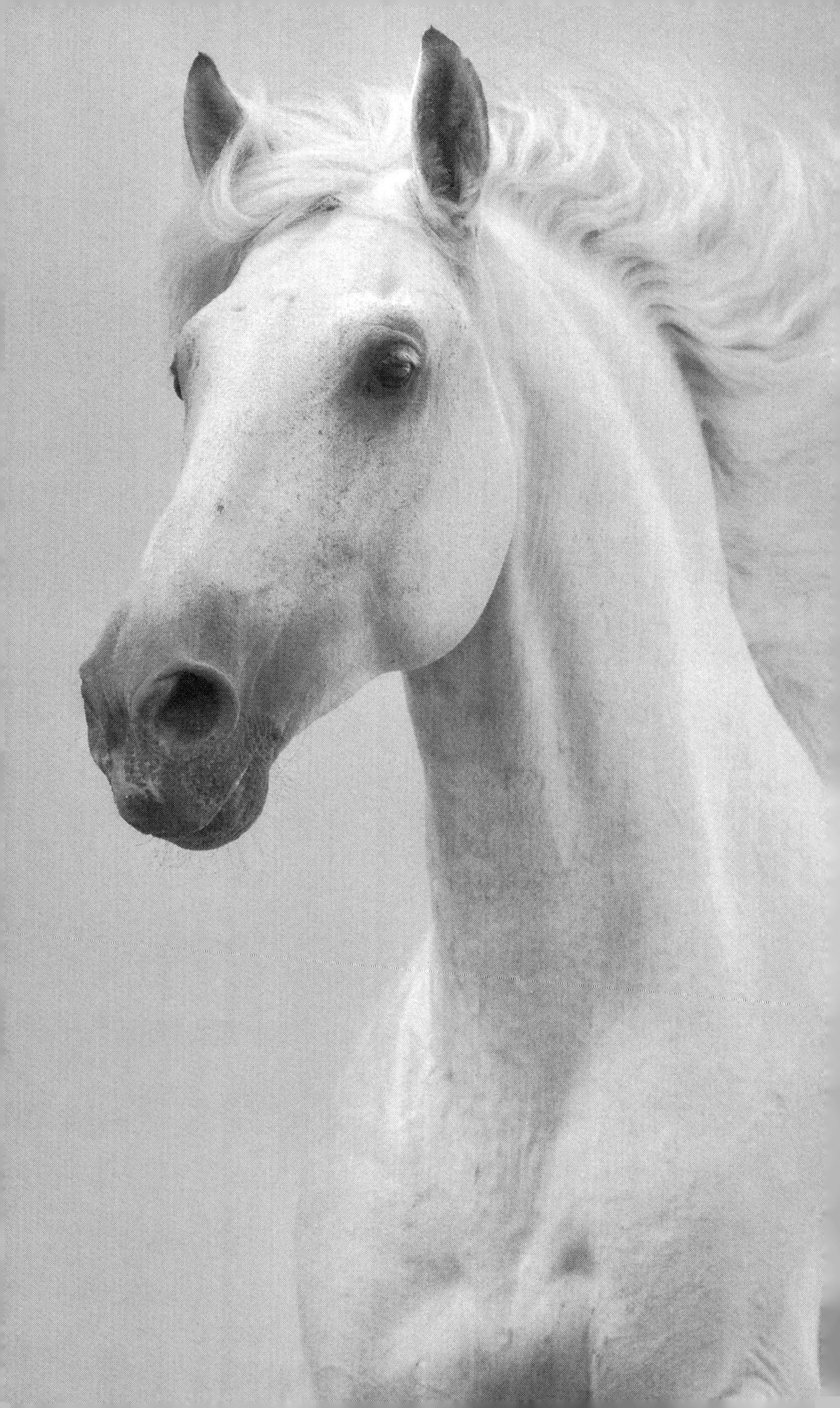

# The White Horse Meditation

Find a comfortable position in which to sit or stand near your horse. Relax your body and your arms and your shoulders and your legs. Place your hands on your lap, feeling your spine nice and straight, so energy can flow easily. If you're separated from your horse, close your eyes; if you are in a paddock or stall with your horse, keep your eyes open in soft focus. Take a nice, deep breath and let it out slowly.

Take another deep breath and let it out. Feel yourself relaxing, letting go of all of your thoughts, the past and the future, and bring all of your awareness to the here and now.

Now, I would like you to take a journey with me. Imagine you're walking through a thick, green forest. It's a sunny day, but cool and quiet amidst the trees. Ferns and wildflowers border the trail you walk upon.

Allow your eyes to take in the tallness of the trees, the shades of green all around you. Allow your ears to hear the sweet songs of birds that fill the air. Allow your nose to inhale the sweet smell of redwoods and pine trees.

As you walk along the path, you begin to hear the sounds of water in the distance, and so you follow these sounds. Soon you discover a small waterfall next to the trail.

You sit down on a nice, flat rock overlooking the tumbling water. It is so peaceful here, and this peace enters your heart. The sun shines brightly through the trees upon you. As you sit here, meditating with the water, you feel as if someone is watching you, and sure enough, as you turn to look behind you, you see a beautiful white horse come forward from the trees.

The horse shines so brightly you can hardly keep her gaze. You can see her wild spirit, and yet because she senses your peaceful heart, she comes closer, approaching to stand just a few feet away as you gaze at each other. You admire her long mane and tail, her delicate, graceful head and ears, her strong feet and liquid brown eyes. She's beautiful, and so bright she reminds you of the sun.

Reach out your hand as the horse walks slowly toward you. As her nose touches your hand, you can feel her energy entering you through your fingers and flowing through your body and to your heart. As you gaze into her deep eyes, it's as if you can sense the world as she does. Your hearing and sense of smell become extremely acute. Even more deeply than her physical senses, you can also feel her spiritual qualities, her wisdom, grace, and speed. She can be calm and still like the earth, or fly like the wind.

With the help of this white horse, you can now travel deeply into your heart. You can look deeply within to view a challenge you are facing right now in your life, a place where you may feel unsure of yourself and unsettled, where you have doubts or a lack of clarity. Perhaps there's a choice or decision you need to make that requires a deep inner wisdom.

This is a decision in your life that will require gentleness and grace for you to succeed. Embrace yourself now with love and compassion, for even if you have struggled for a long time with this challenge, today—in fact, right now, at this moment, with the help of this horse—you are going to be able to move forward in the wisest way possible.

So let your heart open to the horse, and feel the horse's heart open to you as well. Your two hearts begin to shine brighter and brighter and brighter. Within this amazing light, allow yourself to access your own deepest wisdom within your spirit. Feel all outside negative influences or inner instability or worries lose their power. You feel so strong with this bright heart light shining within you, and you realize it is the bright light of wisdom, and this wisdom will effortlessly cast away any shadows, doubts, and fears.

With the support of the horse, you can now see deeper than the surface of this issue. You can see right to its heart, and with the bright light of wisdom shining in your heart, you know exactly what to do.

A deep sense of peace floods through your entire being as you feel yourself accessing your deepest and wisest self, and you know that no matter what challenges life may bring—this challenge right now, or others in the future—you will always be able to cleverly navigate through it all.

So take a moment and sit in the beautiful space of wisdom energy. The energy of the horse envelopes you, strengthening you. Feel the light touching everything about this challenging situation in your life. All will be well, and you know the perfect path to take.

The horse feels your inner shift into wisdom, courage, decisiveness, and clarity. She joyfully whirls and gallops into the forest, beckoning you to join her.

As you move to follow, you suddenly realize you have transformed into her, into the white horse, and your graceful steps are as fast and sure as the wind as you move powerfully through the forest.

As you breathe, you can also inhale the many layers of life and activity in the forest. You realize the forest isn't really a quiet place, as humans often imagine, but in fact, a very busy and active place, with many creatures busily living their lives. Your quick hooves devour the trail as you gallop through the trees, up and down hills.

You jump across a river and pass through some thick trees into a wide, open meadow. The sun shines here, and it is very warm and peaceful. You stop to rest and feel the light of the sun warming you inside and out. Your horse eyes slowly close, to rest.

When you awaken, you're in your human form again, sitting on the rock beside the waterfall. You are still aware of the bright light that is shining in your heart, that light which the horse helped you to rediscover. You're also aware of your new clarity about the challenge in your life right now. You know that you have all the wisdom you need to make the right decision for health, balance, and harmony.

Take a moment to thank the horse for her lesson to you today, for sharing her cleverness, her wisdom, and her open heart. When you're ready, set your intention to finish and take a nice, deep, cleansing breath and slowly come back and open your eyes.

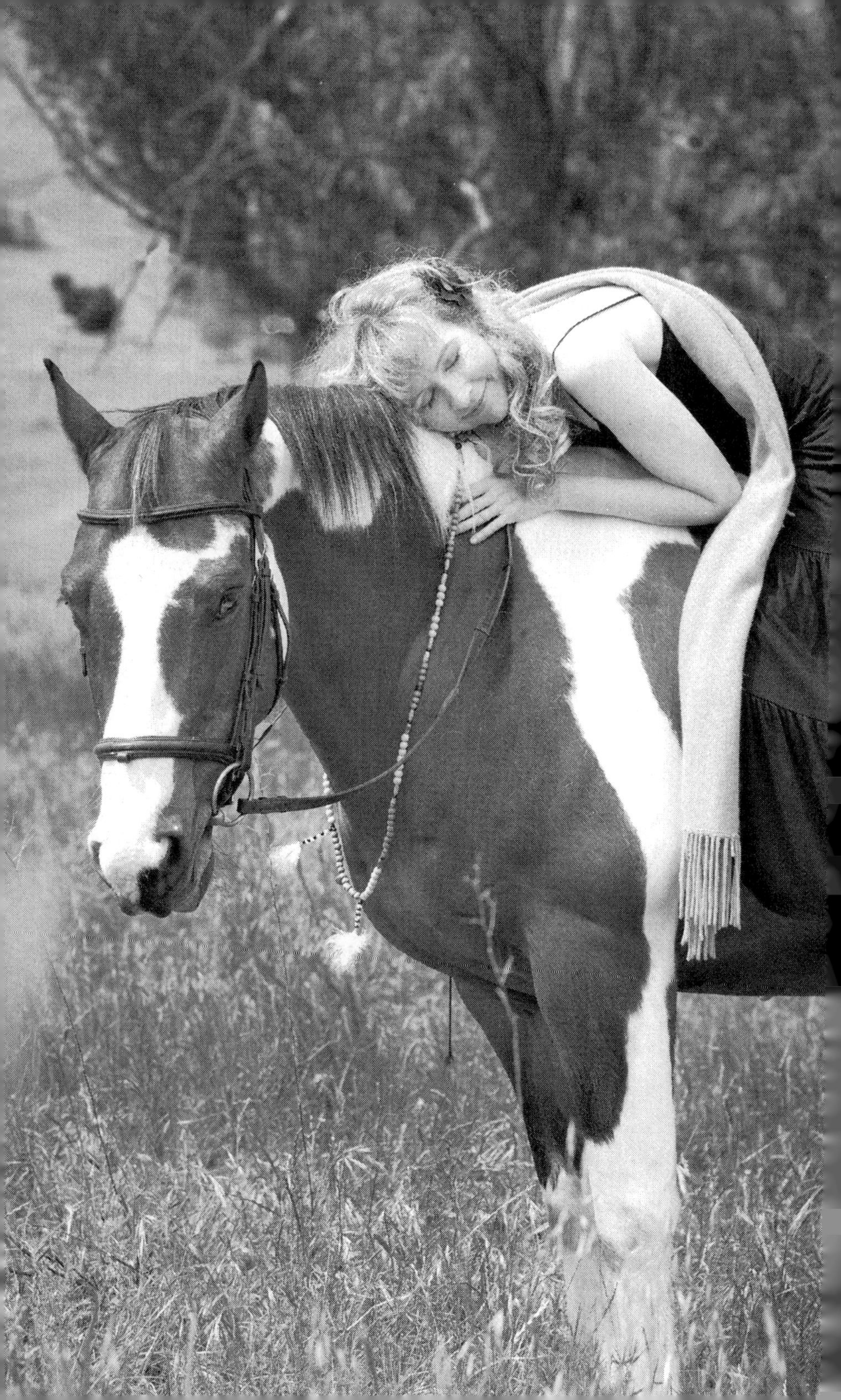

**CHAPTER 15**

# The Healing Power of Compassion and an Open Heart

THROUGHOUT THIS BOOK I have shared many Reiki experiences, techniques and meditations. I encourage you to practice every day if you can; the more you practice, the more you will discover about the meaning of heart to heart healing. Along with the information I've already shared, here are five mindful practices to incorporate into your life each and every day. They may seem simple, but they will help you to experience even deeper heart to heart connections in your equine Reiki journey.

First, begin your day reciting the Reiki precepts: just for today, do not anger; just for today, do not worry; be humble; be honest; be compassionate to yourself and others. Recite them the first thing in the morning and invite your horses to help you to remain mindful of them throughout the day.

Second, volunteer at your local horse sanctuary. The gratitude the horses will show you for your kindness will help you to open your heart. It is not easy work, for you will become more aware of the suffering and sadness that exists in the world. However, with the help of Reiki meditation, you will also become more fully conscious of the power of love and kindness to make things whole. Love and kindness are the most powerful healers in the world, and this is something you will feel with your heart and also see with your eyes. When you spend time with rescued horses, they will teach you the true meaning of compassion.

Third, cultivate compassion between species by contemplating ways that you and your horses are alike. Think about the things that you share not only on the outer level but also on the inner level. Then do this with other species who may cross your path. How are you the same? Contemplation will help you begin to see that although we are many species, we are all living beings, and underneath it all, we share a common soul and spirit. This realization is the foundation for healing our world.

Fourth, practice random acts of kindness to all creatures. Find ways big and small in each and every day to show kindness to the beings around you. Take your dog to his best-loved park. Spend an extra-long time grazing your horse in his favorite spot, or rescue a butterfly from the hot sun. Get in the habit of keeping your eyes open to others: humans, animals, and even the smallest creatures. Set your intent each day to help them in every way you can, and watch a beautiful day of compassion and wonder unfold. Perhaps you begin with one act of kindness a day, but soon you might find yourself helping multiple creatures every single day. What a beautiful way to leave a healing trace wherever you go.

Fifth, as you end your day, take a few minutes to reflect on your day's compassionate service. What heart to heart connections did you make? How did you change a life? What did an animal teach you about life and healing? How does your heart feel when you bring mindful awareness to these compassionate connections?

These five simple practices will enhance your Reiki meditations and create more compassion in your life. This in turn will bring a deeper sense of happiness within you. This inner sense of well-being will shine out into the world, creating healing radiance wherever you go. Before you know it, your heart and the hearts of the horses you connect with will be transformed. This heart to heart healing is what equine Reiki is all about.

The time has come for you to go outside to your horse teachers. They are ready to begin your heart to heart healing lessons. Reiki will help you remember that you already have everything you need to create the perfect healing space: your pure intention to help, your mindful presence in this very moment and the vast, infinite light of your beautiful open heart.

Be light. Be love. Be peace. Be Reiki.

# INDEX OF MEDITATIONS:

Reiki Practice: Horse Hatsurei Ho . . . . . . . . . . . . . . . . . . . . . 15
Rainbow Healing Meditation . . . . . . . . . . . . . . . . . . . . . . . . . 47
Being Peace with Your Horse Meditation . . . . . . . . . . . . . . . 61
The Healing Pond Meditation. . . . . . . . . . . . . . . . . . . . . . . . 75
Spirit Horse Meditation . . . . . . . . . . . . . . . . . . . . . . . . . . . . 89
Pegasus and Courage Meditation. . . . . . . . . . . . . . . . . . . . 105
Sun/Moon Sitting Meditation: . . . . . . . . . . . . . . . . . . . . . . 111
Metta Practice with Horses . . . . . . . . . . . . . . . . . . . . . . . . 112
Walking Meditation with your Horse . . . . . . . . . . . . . . . . 115
The Four Spheres Riding Meditation. . . . . . . . . . . . . . . . . 117
Earth and Sky Meditation with Your Horse. . . . . . . . . . . . 155
Be the Mountain for Your Horse Meditation. . . . . . . . . . . 169
The White Horse Meditation . . . . . . . . . . . . . . . . . . . . . . 181

# ACKNOWLEDGEMENTS

Special thanks to:

Che and Indigo Prasad, for supporting me every day, so that I can do the work that I do.

Susan Pommer, my dressage trainer, for all she has taught me about the "art" of riding with intuition, respect and sensitivity. What I have learned from you has enhanced my understanding of heart to heart connections.

Leah D'Ambrosio for your partnership in SARA and strong Reiki friendship. Our travels around the world to share Reiki with animals are some of my most precious memories!

Frans Stiene for encouraging me to dive more deeply into the essence of Reiki practice.

Gail and Richard Pope for opening your home at BrightHaven to me as well as my Reiki students for so many years. I have learned so much from your philosophy as well as the horses and other animals of BrightHaven!

Ann Noyce and Carrie Higdon for your loving support and assistance in editing the manuscript. You rock!

Lexie Cataldo for your talent in taking amazing photos that capture the spirit of equine Reiki.

Joyce Leonard for the original idea to use the healing pond as an image for meditation: just beautiful!

# ABOUT THE AUTHOR

Kathleen Prasad is founder of Animal Reiki Source, offering Animal Reiki sessions and training programs to animal lovers, veterinarians, animal care professionals, shelter and sanctuary staff and volunteers around the world. She is also cofounder and president of the Shelter Animal Reiki Association (SARA), the first nonprofit of its kind, promoting the use of Reiki meditation in animal shelters, sanctuaries and rescues worldwide. SARA's educational program spans the globe, with members across the U.S., as well as in Canada, Europe, India and Australia. Kathleen has taught Reiki to the staff and volunteers of many animal organizations, including BrightHaven, Remus Memorial Horse Sanctuary, The CARE Foundation, Best Friends Animal Society, the San Francisco SPCA and Guide Dogs for the Blind.

Originally trained in Reiki in 1998, Kathleen now studies with Frans Stiene of the International House of Reiki, a school teaching traditional Japanese Reiki techniques and philosophy. A global leader in the animal Reiki profession, Kathleen has authored the *Animal Reiki Practitioner Code of Ethics*, *Reiki for Dogs*, *Everything Animal Reiki* and *5 Powerful Meditations to Help Heal Your Animals*, as well as co-authored the books *The Animal Reiki Handbook* and *Animal Reiki: Using Energy to Heal the Animals in Your Life*. She has been published in magazines such as *The Journal of the American Holistic Veterinary Association*, *Natural Horse Magazine*, *Equine Wellness Magazine* and has been featured in many radio and TV programs. Visit Kathleen online at www.AnimalReikiSource.com.

Made in the USA
Lexington, KY
25 January 2017